TRACING YOUR BOER WAR ANCESTORS

FAMILY HISTORY FROM PEN & SWORD

Tracing Secret Service Ancestors

Tracing Your Air Force Ancestors

Tracing Your Ancestors

Tracing Your Ancestors from 1066 to 1837

Tracing Your Ancestors Through Death Records

Tracing Your Ancestors Through Family Photographs

Tracing Your Ancestors Using the Census

Tracing Your Ancestors' Childhood

Tracing Your Ancestors' Parish Records

Tracing Your Aristocratic Ancestors

Tracing Your Army Ancestors – 2nd Edition

Tracing Your Birmingham Ancestors

Tracing Your Black Country Ancestors

Tracing Your British Indian Ancestors

Tracing Your Canal Ancestors

Tracing Your Channel Islands Ancestors

Tracing Your Coalmining Ancestors

Tracing Your Criminal Ancestors

Tracing Your East Anglian Ancestors

Tracing Your East End Ancestors

Tracing Your Edinburgh Ancestors

Tracing Your First World War Ancestors

Tracing Your Great War Ancestors: The Gallipoli Campaign

Tracing Your Great War Ancestors: The Somme

Tracing Your Great War Ancestors: Ypres

Tracing Your Huguenot Ancestors

Tracing Your Jewish Ancestors

Tracing Your Labour Movement Ancestors

Tracing Your Lancashire Ancestors

Tracing Your Leeds Ancestors

Tracing Your Legal Ancestors

Tracing Your Liverpool Ancestors

Tracing Your London Ancestors

Tracing Your Medical Ancestors

Tracing Your Merchant Navy Ancestors

Tracing Your Naval Ancestors

Tracing Your Northern Ancestors

Tracing Your Pauper Ancestors

Tracing Your Police Ancestors

Tracing Your Prisoner of War Ancestors: The First World War

Tracing Your Railway Ancestors

Tracing Your Royal Marine Ancestors

Tracing Your Rural Ancestors

Tracing Your Scottish Ancestors

Tracing Your Second World War Ancestors

Tracing Your Servant Ancestors

Tracing Your Service Women Ancestors

Tracing Your Shipbuilding Ancestors

Tracing Your Tank Ancestors

Tracing Your Textile Ancestors

Tracing Your Trade and Craftsmen Ancestors

Tracing Your Welsh Ancestors

Tracing Your West Country Ancestors

Tracing Your Yorkshire Ancestors

TRACING YOUR BOER WAR ANCESTORS

Soldiers of a Forgotten War

Jane Marchese Robinson

Pen & Sword
FAMILY HISTORY

First published in Great Britain in 2016
PEN & SWORD FAMILY HISTORY
an imprint of
Pen & Sword Books Ltd
47 Church Street,
Barnsley
South Yorkshire,
S70 2AS

Copyright © Jane Marchese Robinson, 2016

ISBN 978 1 47382 242 9

The right of Jane Robinson to be identified as Author of this Work has been asserted by her in accordance with the Copyright, Designs and Patents Act 1988.

A CIP catalogue record for this book is available from the British Library.

All rights reserved. No part of this book may be reproduced or transmitted in any form or by any means, electronic or mechanical including photocopying, recording or by any information storage and retrieval system, without permission from the Publisher in writing.

Typeset in Palatino by CHIC GRAPHICS

Printed and bound in England by
CPI Group (UK), Croydon, CR0 4YY

Pen & Sword Books Ltd incorporates the imprints of Pen & Sword Archaeology, Atlas, Aviation, Battleground, Discovery, Family History, History, Maritime, Military, Naval, Politics, Railways, Select, Social History, Transport, True Crime, Claymore Press, Frontline Books, Leo Cooper, Praetorian Press, Remember When, Seaforth Publishing and Wharncliffe.

For a complete list of Pen & Sword titles please contact
PEN & SWORD BOOKS LTD
47 Church Street, Barnsley, South Yorkshire, S70 2AS, England
E-mail: enquiries@pen-and-sword.co.uk
Website: www.pen-and-sword.co.uk

CONTENTS

List of Plates		vi
Foreword		1
Chapter 1	A Tale of Two Wars	4
Chapter 2	'It'll All Be Over by Christmas'	11
Chapter 3	The Call for Volunteers and the Besieged Towns	33
Chapter 4	The War at Home	65
Chapter 5	The Sickness Took Them	74
Chapter 6	And the Boys Went Too	83
Chapter 7	The Bitter End	89
Chapter 8	'A Land Fit for Heroes'?	101
Chapter 9	Suffer Little Children	121
Chapter 10	They Served and Many Served Again	137
Afterword		154
Looking For Your Boer War Ancestor		156
Acknowledgements		165
Notes		168
Bibliography		172
Index		173

LIST OF PLATES

Albert Skedgell. *(Courtesy of Roy Tucker)*
George Ravenhill was awarded the VC at the Battle of Colenso. *(Courtesy of Graham Knight)*
The HMS *Doris* Memorial in Devonport Park, Plymouth. *(Courtesy of Tony Marchese)*
A street in Nechells, Birmingham, the area where George Ravenhill lived. *(Courtesy of Graham Knight)*
Fred Griffin from Honiton, Devon. *(Courtesy of Jenny Ridd)*
Robert Slattery from Lancashire. *(Courtesy of Maureen Noonan)*
Henry Gardner from Bermondsey died at Intombi Hospital near Ladysmith. *(Courtesy of John Shalice)*
First page of the letter to Henry's mother informing her of his death. *(Courtesy of John Shalice)*
Charles Dunn, a young soldier in the Coldstream Guards who died at Standerton Hospital. *(Courtesy of David Yabsley)*
Lizzie Bowcombe, Charles's girlfriend. *(Courtesy of David Yabsley)*
British soldiers entering Pretoria in June 1900. *(Courtesy of Western Cape Archives and Library, Cape Town)*
Boy soldier after the Battle of Colesberg. *(Courtesy of the National Media Museum, Science and Society Picture Library)*
Robert Milburn, the author's great-uncle, as a young recruit to the Coldstream Guards. *(Courtesy of Mary Ann Parkinson)*
Robert pictured with soldiers from the Queen Victoria's Black Watch Guard. *(Courtesy of Mary Ann Parkinson)*
Boer women guarding their belongings. *(Courtesy of Sheila Ashford)*
'Destroyed Boer Farmhouse'. *(Courtesy of Professor Sir Roderick Floud, from Liddell Hart Centre for Military Archives)*
William Duncan, aged five, at school in Dundee. *(Courtesy of Malcolm Duncan)*
His father, William Neilson Duncan. *(Courtesy of Malcolm Duncan)*
A ring made from South African gold brought back by John Ball for his sweetheart Bessie. *(Courtesy of Nicola Wills)*
John Ball's son Steve and wife: the family still treasures the ring. *(Courtesy of Nicola Wills)*
Medals awarded to Tom Randell of the Royal Artillery. *(Courtesy of Robert Wall)*

DEDICATION

For my friend Maggie Grant (1940–2013) whose advice
and support was always invaluable.
I'm sorry she won't be able to see this published.

FOREWORD

The inspiration for this book arose in 2006 when I inherited an autograph book belonging to my Belgian grandmother. She had collected many signatures and drawings from foreign visitors whilst working at the Strand Palace Hotel in London from 1919 onwards. This led to me researching her history and trying to discover whether she was one of the 250,000 Belgian refugees who fled their homeland when the Germans invaded in 1914.

I explored archives in this country and in Belgium. In London I searched workhouse records from 1914. Sadly I could not find her. However, in the London Metropolitan archives I did discover an English family consisting of a mother and four children, one daughter of whom had a different surname. Coincidentally I had been looking for a theme for a novel and this family became my inspiration: what circumstances led this girl to have been living with this family? The daughter had been born in 1902, at the end of the Boer War, and I imagined that she was the result of a relationship her mother had while her husband was away fighting in South Africa.

I had studied history at school and had undertaken a university degree in social history and yet I had not been taught anything about the Boer War. Therefore I needed to undertake considerable research in order to 'flesh out' my story. This included reading about the workhouses during this period and extensive research about this war.

A synopsis of the novel was submitted to Pen and Sword publishers when something unexpected happened. They suggested that I write a non-fiction book concerning the ordinary soldiers of the war and what support they or their families received afterwards in a world without a welfare state. The book was to contain real-life testimonies, a veritable challenge when those men and their direct families had died a long time ago. Diaries in archives provided considerable illumination but contacting regional newspapers, with a request for personal stories, yielded greater results. I was privileged to receive many stories, letters and photographs of this almost forgotten war. I have tried to include as many as possible in this book in order to throw a light on those men who fought and died in the heat 6,000 miles from home and to recall the hardships many women and children suffered as a direct result. Widowed or caring for a disabled husband, times were tough for the ordinary soldier's family.

Understanding this conflict required journeys to South Africa and visits to places away from the usual tourist routes, such as Bethlehem, Bloemfontein and Wakkerstroom. There I elicited some interesting oral history from the Afrikaner families who were descendants of those affected by the war and the results of the British 'Scorched Earth' policy. Visits to the battle sites at Groenkop, Spion Kop and Magersfontein led to a greater awareness and knowledge of the horrors of the war suffered by the soldiers.

In almost every town and village in this country there is a granite cross listing local men who died in both world wars. There seems to be nothing to remember the men of the Boer War who fought and died only twelve years before: that is, until you start looking! From the north of Scotland to Penzance in West Cornwall there are memorials in all shapes and sizes; from the imposing memorial in Cannon Hill Park, Birmingham, to an actual gun that was captured in South Africa in Devonport Park, Plymouth. All list names of those who died. The memorials are not just in outside venues, many churches have plaques usually in gleaming brass listing three or four local men who died. These show that this conflict affected every part of the country and that

Foreword

the Boer War deceased were commemorated at the time. In the end, most unexpectedly, my family research came full circle when I discovered some documents that drew me to look at the 1901 census for my father's family. Seeing that my great-aunt was recorded in the census with a baby, but that her husband was absent. I was able to discover that my great-uncle by marriage had served in the Boer War with the Coldstream Guards. After so many other people had shared their relatives' story I had finally found out that my family also had one to tell!

Chapter 1

A TALE OF TWO WARS

2014 saw the anniversary of the start of the First World War. The conflict, variously called the Great War and the 'War to end all Wars', was to be commemorated widely both in this country and across Europe. The battles that took place in Europe and Asia Minor led to the deaths of unprecedented numbers of people. Some ten million soldiers and seven million civilians perished and twenty million were wounded. Simmering feuds between the powers of Europe over territorial disputes, competition for the rich pickings of African colonies and rivalry between power blocs seeking expanded spheres of influence brought about this conflict that saw carnage of unimaginable proportions. Young men fought and died in trenches filled with mud which swallowed the bodies of their comrades and attracted rats to eat them. Many were never recovered and their bodies lie forever somewhere below the surface of the Belgian and Northern French countryside. Men wounded in the conflict were often so severely maimed that they could neither work nor do anything socially useful afterwards. Some 80,000 British soldiers were officially recognised to have suffered from shell shock but many more remained undiagnosed and were considered 'malingerers', deserters or just cowards, for which the punishment was death by firing squad. We know all this and much more besides since this war has been written about and filmed more than any other conflict. In the 1960s the BBC produced the television series *The Great War* which traced the conflict from its outbreak to the final peace treaty. Running for twenty-six episodes, it illustrated the massive enthusiasm shown by volunteers at the declaration of war and subsequent events, including the horror of trench warfare up until the 1918 Armistice. It mesmerised a whole generation of viewers and became a fantastic educative tool. The sad soldier on sentry duty beside a trench is the iconic image of the series.

A great many films have been made about this war: *Gallipoli*, *All Quiet on the Western Front* and *A Farewell to Arms* are just three powerful dramas that depict its horrors. Novels abound with many being made into films or plays. Sebastian Faulks's play based on his novel *Birdsong* toured the UK during 2014 powerfully depicting the desolation of a young man's life in the trenches compared to his love affair in pre-war France.

The conflict also saw the creation of some of the most evocative poetry of the twentieth century. As the horrors unfolded poets like John McCrae, Siegfried Sassoon, Edward Thomas, Laurence Binyon and Wilfred Owen conjured up the desperation of life in the trenches. Owen's *Anthem for Doomed Youth*, written when he was convalescing with shell shock, conveys both in words and in its metre a profound sadness as he asks 'What passing bells for those who die as cattle?' Much of this poetry is studied now as part of school syllabuses.

All of these memorials are, as they should be, to remind people of the terrible cataclysm that affected the peoples of Europe and beyond between 1914 and 1918. Far from being the 'War to end all Wars' it harboured the seeds that led to other conflicts not least of which was the Second World War. However, by contrast, British troops had fought in a conflict thousands of miles from home a mere fifteen years earlier during the Boer War. The centenary for that war was in 1999 but its commemoration in this country was almost mute. Indeed it was overshadowed by the Solar Eclipse in August of that year.

This book is about this earlier, eclipsed war and in particular the effect on those who fought, died or were injured for the British

Empire thousands of miles from home. It will seek to examine how the country, so pleased to see regular soldiers and volunteers go to fight the Boers, treated them and their families when they didn't return or when they returned too injured to earn a living. It will look at the plight of the war widows and children orphaned by the conflict. It is a question pertinent for all wars but particularly so in the early 1900s when support for those unable to work was either through the Poor Law or some form of charity. The nature of this war means that its heroes and victims are little known. This book will seek to bring those forgotten men and their families out of the shadows in order to chart and celebrate their lives.

The Boer War, otherwise known as the South African or Anglo-Boer War, began less than three months before the end of the nineteenth century. It was a century that was dominated by one person, Queen Victoria, then the longest-reigning monarch in British history. The Queen commanded an Empire that stretched from New Zealand in the east to Canada in the west encompassing many countries in between. African countries were important to Britain but India was considered the 'Jewel in the Crown'. The Empire fuelled the economy of Britain, providing raw materials for her industry and markets for her goods. Having an empire required a ready supply of resources and it sought to capitalise on new sources of wealth. This could, and indeed did, lead to conflicts with other powers and with the inhabitants of those countries. So it was in South Africa.

Dying in January 1901, Queen Victoria never saw the end of the war. It finished in May 1902 with a British victory but it was not a happy one. Approximately 250,000 British and Commonwealth troops were sent to fight this war. Of the 20,000 British soldiers who died in the war over half succumbed to enteric fever (typhoid), an illness caused by contaminated water, while 22,000 men would return home injured, some permanently disabled. On the other side some 26,000 Boer civilians, mainly young children, died of disease in the concentration camps established by the British and it is now recognised that at least 14,000 black and native peoples died in similar camps. The conflict once dubbed 'The Last Gentleman's War' was in fact far from that.

At home the nineteenth century had seen many advances and developments. The first photograph was taken in 1838, just a year after Victoria became queen. Developments in transport enabled an unprecedented speed of travel. In 1825 the first railway line was inaugurated. In 1839 Isambard Kingdom Brunel launched the first paddle steamer and in 1845 smoother road travel became a possibility with the invention of tarmacadam providing a hard surface for road building. In 1863 an underground railway powered by steam was opened in London. These developments enabled the movement of goods and people vital to the expansion of industry. Concrete was invented in 1849. It was a cheap material and opened up many possibilities for building. From rubber tyres to petrol and from sewing machines to typewriters during Victoria's reign Britain saw unprecedented advances which stoked the economy whilst at the same time making work easier.

A major development in this period was the provision of universal, though not compulsory, education through Forster's Education Act of 1870. Ten years later it became compulsory for children between the ages of five and ten, though some parents still kept their children out of school to earn money for the family. Educating working-class children was a major advance and it meant that the soldiers who went to the Boer War were, in the main, literate. It was the first war in which ordinary soldiers could write home with an account of the conflict and many records of this survive. The newly expanding popular press sent reporters to cover the conflict, the most famous of whom was Winston Churchill. Indeed letters home from soldiers refer to the fact that their relatives will probably have read about particular battles in the paper. Film footage too was provided through newsreels and seen in cinemas. There was no shortage of written and visual testimony for this war.

In stark contrast to these positive developments it is known that almost 40 per cent of volunteers for the war were found unfit to serve. Young men brought up in impoverished city neighbourhoods were stunted in their growth. Country boys too had suffered as a result of a long agricultural recession. The working classes had had some benefits from the advances in Victorian society but life for most was one of grinding poverty. With no ability to control the size of their families it was a struggle to feed their children. It was hard to find work and when found wages were generally pitiful. Keeping a job was equally difficult since work was often of a seasonal nature and there was no employment protection. When there was no work there was no support available other than through the dreaded workhouse. So people eked a living as best they could sorting rubbish, waiting on the dockside to be picked for casual labour and many women and girls sold themselves on city streets. And thus it was that many young men joined the army

A number of social commentators investigated the conditions of the poorest classes at this time. The clergy of various denominations often made ministering to the poor part of their mission. In 1883 in the rather dramatically-titled *The Bitter Cry of Outcast London*[1] (published by the London Congregational Union) the Reverend Andrew Mearns visited slum housing in the Bermondsey and Deptford areas of London. Of Bermondsey he wrote: 'Few who read these pages have any conception of what these pestilential human rookeries are, where thousands are crowded together amidst horrors which call to mind what we have heard of the middle passage of the slave ship.'

'Every room in these reeking tenements houses a family, often two. In one cellar a sanitary inspector reports finding a father, mother, three children and four pigs. In another room a missionary found a man, ill with small pox, his wife just recovering from her eighth confinement and the children running about half naked and covered with dirt.' In Deptford he found further evidence of poverty: 'Another apartment which contains father, mother and six children, two of whom are ill with scarlet fever. Here is a mother who turns her children into the street in the early evening because she lets her room for immoral purposes until long after midnight, when the poor little wretches creep back again if they have not found some miserable shelter elsewhere.'

There was no form of social security or pensions. If people could not work for whatever reason the only support was through the Poor Law which usually meant being admitted to the workhouse. The Poor Law of 1834 had instituted a draconian form of poor relief where admission to the workhouse meant children being separated from their parents and husbands from wives. Rations were poor and tedious, and often backbreaking work was enforced on inmates. Over the century various scandals erupted in workhouses where masters starved inmates, pocketing the surplus monies for themselves. Tales of savage beatings also emerged. Poor people dreaded the places which were nicknamed 'Bastilles' and they would try all means to avoid admission.

Working for the rich and titled formed a major form of employment in these times. All big houses had servants and the richer the household the more servants were employed. Many of the lower-level servants were recruited from the workhouses and orphanages, swapping one form of drudgery for another. Television dramas such as *Upstairs Downstairs* romanticised, to a degree, the life of servants. They do not show the girls who worked from five in the morning until ten or eleven at night scrubbing, polishing and carrying heavy pails of water, so exhausted by the end of their day that they could barely stand up.[2]

Yet it was the sons of these titled households, educated at public schools, who became army officers. In South Africa during the Boer War their lack of fighting experience often put their men in danger. These young officers themselves were indoctrinated with a sense of adventure and jingoism but the deference of the times meant that their judgement could not be questioned.

In brief then, this was the world experienced by so many at the time when British troops sailed off to South Africa to fight for their Queen and Empire. The conditions they were to experience in the South African veldt, with searing hot days and freezing nights, not to mention the threat of wild animals, were as different from London, Leeds or Dundee as could be imagined. How those soldiers fared in this environment, how many returned and the effect on their families when they didn't return is the subject of this book.

Chapter 2

'IT'LL ALL BE OVER BY CHRISTMAS'

The war started in October 1899. In Britain at that time it was referred to as the South African War. It is important to note that name if you are looking into newspapers of the time for news of events, regiments, towns or people. The term 'Boer War' only evolved later. 'Boer' means farmer in Dutch and Afrikaans, the language that had evolved from that of the original Dutch settlers who colonised the eastern parts of South Africa during the seventeenth and eighteenth century. Contemporary references are as likely to refer to the Dutch as the Boers. The Boers called the war the 'Tweedevryheidoorlog' or the 'Second Freedom War' from which it can be seen how they regarded the British as their subjugators.

The indigenous peoples of the country were the various black tribes and groupings whose interests and rights had been eroded by the white settlers over several centuries. Both Dutch and English peoples had come to settle in South Africa from the seventeenth century onwards. Both were expanding trading nations which had active outposts in the Far East. The abolition of slavery in the British Empire in the 1830s threatened the free black labour the Boers had come to rely on and enjoy, so they decided to move northwards from the Cape. Being a predominantly farming people, they hoped these lands would offer them fruitful opportunities. However, these lands were already populated by the proud Zulu people and the Boers' journey northwards brought the two groups into bloody conflict. This journey undertaken across vast expanses in ox-drawn wagons has become known as 'The Great Trek' and has taken on a mythic quality in the Afrikaner psyche.

Eventually, after monumental journeys, they had settled north of the Vaal River; later named the Transvaal, this was an area which, initially, the English were not interested in colonising themselves. Later it was the British interest in their territory that would lead to both the first and second Boer Wars. At the time British foreign policy was focused on bringing the whole of South Africa under their control. So in 1879 they launched an attack on the Zulu nation. This particular conflict is best known to cinema goers through the film *Zulu* in which the British, having been trounced at Islandlwana, mounted a courageous defence against overwhelming odds of the mission station at Rorke's Drift. Ultimately though the British fought back and at Ulundi the Zulus were vanquished. The Boers had been hemmed in by the Zulu nation and so their defeat would seem to have been to their advantage. However, the Boers' jubilation was short-lived as, boosted by this success, the British went on to declare their sovereignty over the two Boer republics which had then been established, namely The Transvaal and the Orange Free State. The Boers were very unhappy at this turn of events, hence in 1880, under the political leadership of Paul Kruger, they rose up against the British. The First Boer War saw the Boers inflicting three defeats on the British Army. The final one, at Majuba Hill on 27 February 1881 on the border with Natal, was a rout, a resounding victory for the Boers. The British withdrew and cobbled together a treaty whereby the Boers were given control over their internal affairs but the British would decide all foreign policy. It was the beginning of a real rift between the Boers and Great Britain. Majuba was often quoted mockingly by Boer troops against the British in the Second Boer War. Many of those British soldiers who fought there felt humiliated by the order to withdraw so quickly.

'It'll All Be Over by Christmas'

Of interest, an elderly Afrikaans man, Chris Smit (who, until recently, ran an historical museum in Wakkerstroom, Mpumalanga, South Africa, and who I met on a visit in 2013) believed that it was Queen Victoria who never forgave the Boers for the defeat at Majuba. The legacy of such conflicts lingers in the memories of the descendants of local people.

It was just six years after this first war when an event happened that was to change the fortunes and the politics of the Transvaal forever. In 1886 gold was discovered in the Witwatersrand near Johannesburg. It was not long before it was realised that this was the most valuable find ever made anywhere in the world. Prospectors poured in from all over the world to seek their fortune. The majority came from Great Britain, with newspapers advertising weekly passages from Southampton to dig for gold. The Boers called these people, who arrived to prospect for gold, 'Uitlanders', the Dutch word for foreigners. The British government saw that these Britons were contributing to the economy in the Transvaal yet had no say in its governance and hence from London arose a campaign to give these Uitlanders the right to vote there.

Whilst this campaign was initially a war of words, in 1895 an adventurer called Leander Jameson, in conjunction with Cecil Rhodes, then Prime Minister of the Cape Colony, and with the tacit support of Joseph Chamberlain MP and others, organised an armed raid on Johannesburg. The assumption was that the Uitlanders would rise to his support to claim their rights and overthrow the Transvaal government. However, their support was not forthcoming, perhaps because they were more concerned with mining gold than gaining any political rights.

Evidently this excursion, later to be known as the 'Jameson Raid', was a miscalculation in more ways than one. It gave an amazing boost to the Transvaal President Paul Kruger, whose popularity had been waning, and it saw Jameson and other plotters shipped back to London to be tried in the High Court.

Sentences of up to fifteen months in gaol were handed out and Rhodes was exposed as one of the chief organisers behind the whole adventure.

Since the discovery of gold in the Witwatersrand, commonly known as the Rand, the British had been looking to extend their influence northwards from the Cape and Natal. Agitation for the Uitlander franchise was one way. The more direct way was in the months leading up to the war and, anticipating conflict, British army units totalling 10,662 men had already been shipped to South Africa. Combined with locally-raised troops the British military in the country numbered 27,550. Of these 18,000 were in the province of Natal in the south-east. The Boers had asked that British troops withdraw south of the Natal border, which was agreed. However, the demand that that no further British troops be landed was not. It was precisely this demand, that Britain could not agree to, which was to be the trigger for the conflict. The war started on 11 October 1899.

It was expected to be over quickly since a bunch of Boer farmers were thought to be no match for the British Empire, with its superior firepower and standing army. The army command was determined that they would not be beaten by the Boers as they had been in 1881. The phrase 'It'll be over by Christmas' was first used at this time. Two and a half months seemed plenty of time in which to beat them. Christmas in Britain today is one of the most important annual festivals. However, it is worth reflecting that at the beginning of the nineteenth century it was hardly celebrated. Traditions brought over by Queen Victoria's German husband, Albert, combined with the popularity of Dickens's *A Christmas Carol* (published in 1843) raised its profile significantly. Sweets in crackers, families gathering round the tree and Christmas cards (eleven and a half million were produced in 1880 alone) were all growing manifestations of the pleasures of the season. The allure of spending Christmas at home created a warm image and one which the soldiers fighting on the veldt

'It'll All Be Over by Christmas'

would have looked forward to. As in the Great War, when this rallying call was proclaimed, it was something for soldiers and anxious families in Britain to embrace.

The earliest engagements of the Second Boer War, at Talana Hill and Elandslaagte, were British victories but not without loss of life. One of the principal regiments fighting at Elandslaagte was the Gordon Highlanders. Scotland had historically provided many men for the British army and many now fought in the Boer War. Elandslaagte took place the day after the Battle of Talana. It was usual for troops to rest and recover between battles. After Talana the troops were in their camp, resting up and repairing their kit. The Scottish regiments wore kilts, so for them this meant covering their black and white sporrans with khaki material and trying to camouflage their white webbing with a mixture of brown paint and cow dung. When their officer, Captain Buchanan, ran down the ranks at lunchtime exhorting them to prepare for battle the day after Talana, many soldiers laughed. They didn't believe him. It was true, however, since Boer commandoes had been seen cutting the telegraph wires that served the town of Dundee up the line. It would have been a strange coincidence for many of the soldiers for whom Dundee in Scotland was their home town.

So within an hour the various regiments were sent on a train in the direction of Elandslaagte near where the Boer commandoes were encamped, hidden amongst several kopjes. How to surmount or pass through the South African kopjes became the pattern in this war. When the Boers started a volley of bullets the Gordon Highlanders, in particular were a target; their dark green kilts stood out against the colour of the veldt. The black and white sporrans which they had not had time to cover became a target for the crack Boer sharpshooters. The battle raged all day and became more violent as a dark African storm clouded visibility around five o'clock in the afternoon. At this point the Gordon Highlanders and other regiments were stumbling in semi-darkness across a rock strewn landscape trying to find a target.

Many died and were wounded on both sides and the finale was when the cavalry went in with sabres and lances. The Boers were retreating and took heavy losses. They and their African retainers were left speared on the ground; a terrible sight.

A young private called **Edward Printy**, a Gordon Highlander from the town of Dundee, lost his life that day. As with many of his comrades across the country, Edward came from a poor industrialised area of his city. His widowed mother and sisters had worked in the jute mills and he, himself, had worked as a rivet beater in a local mill. The *Dundee Courier* reported his death on 25 October 1899, remarking that his late father had been a soldier and through his involvement with the Perthshire Militia he had been encouraged to join up in August 1894 at the age of eighteen. As in many similar reports of the time the poignancy for his family was underlined by the knowledge that just days before his death they had written to him with hopeful messages. He was the only boy in his family and was just twenty-three when he died.

The Battle of Rietfontein on 24 October was fought to try and take a ridge of strategic hills from the Boers and in this it failed miserably. A letter home to parents published in the *Staines and Egham News* in November 1899 gives this account:

> Dear father and mother. Just a few lines which I trust will find you quite well as I am thankful to say it leaves me at present. On Tuesday last 24th we were in action for the first time. We marched away from camp about 4.15 am. We had proceeded about 7 miles when we were ordered to attack the enemy. My company was the first to leave leading the way across some open fields. We had not got very far before the enemy opened fire on us with their artillery . . . As we neared their position the rifle bullets fell round us like hailstones. I will not attempt to describe the fight, it was too horrible. No one can form any idea of the battlefield

'It'll All Be Over by Christmas'

unless he has experienced it. We lost our Colonel and about ten men killed and 54 wounded and yet there we were smoking our pipes as cool as ever not knowing but what the next shot might carry us off.

On 9 December he wrote again describing what we would nowadays call a surreal incident relating to the battle: 'There was a curious thing at the fight at Rietfontein. Several ladies turned up on bicycles. Of course they kept a long distance off but one of the enemy's shells pitched quite close to them which sent them pedalling off to a safer position where they took cover behind rocks as if they were born to it. Very plucky of them, though they were rather in the way.'[1] This restrained description provides a sense of polite Victorian values. The soldiers must really have been incredulous that these women had come for a spectacle without thinking of the risks not just for them but for the soldiers.

By the end of October 1899 the strategic town of Ladysmith near Durban was besieged by the Boers with a unit of British troops holed up there. In early November the diamond town of Kimberley and that of Mafeking both in the north-west of the country succumbed to the same fate. The army had to lift all three of these sieges; a task which occupied the soldiers for all of the early months of the war.

They were assisted throughout the war by the Royal Navy who shipped in heavy guns by sea, landing at Simonstown. These guns were then moved by railway or sometimes more incredibly by the manpower of young recruits hauling them overland. A memorial in Devonport Park, Plymouth, commemorates the men from one such ship, HMS *Doris*, who died during the war. One survivor was **Albert Skedgell** from Kingsbridge in Devon. He was the youngest sailor to be landed with the Naval Brigades. He took part in no less than thirty-two battles and was awarded clasps for Belfast, Diamond Hill, Johannesburg, Driefontein, Paardeberg, Modder River and Belmont. He was one of the few to be awarded seven clasps. Clearly a much-loved grandfather, his grandson has written a small book about his life. Albert's father worked on a tea clipper which traded round the British Isles and despite his parents trying to dissuade him from this harsh life he was determined to go to sea. He joined the Royal Navy and sailed for South Africa at the beginning of the war. In a similar vein to many others. he recounts the hardships of sleeping on bare ground in the open air and adds that every morning they shook out their blankets carefully as frequently a snake would uncoil from them at the same time.

At the end of November 1899 Albert's naval brigade was with other units on the way to relieve Kimberley. On 25 November his commander saw that the Boers were on a kopje overlooking Belmont station. Albert took part in the fierce battle that ensued and from Belmont they moved on the next day to Graspan. The British won these battles but with many casualties. Their Captain Prothero was badly wounded. When the stretcher-bearers were collecting the dead and tending to the wounded Albert remembered the cries for water from the parched men. November in South Africa is of course the beginning of their hot summer. During the war thirst was an enormous factor for most soldiers and his grandson recounts the memory which meant that he would never waste water even through a dripping tap.

In trying to lift these sieges worse was to come. Beginning on 11 December Britain lost three major battles in one week. From Magersfontein in the north-west to Colenso in the east and Stormberg junction down in the Cape they were defeated. The shock both in South Africa and back in Britain was palpable. The Battle of Magersfontein was intended to lift the siege of Kimberley and, once again, involved a large contingent of Scottish soldiers. To reach the battlefield the soldiers had marched all night in a strong storm over a rocky terrain. Arriving tired, as day broke they had expected to see the Boers charging down the hill to attack them but the enemy was out of sight, hidden in well

'It'll All Be Over by Christmas'

prepared trenches waiting to open fire on the British troops on their arrival. The cold and rain of the night march before had been replaced by the soaring temperatures of the South African summer. These extremes of temperature, unknown to British troops, were an ongoing feature of this war affecting the men often dressed in unsuitable uniforms. At the Battle of Modder River just two days earlier men had had to lie prone for many hours. Wearing the traditional kilts of the Highland regiments many had suffered severely sunburnt legs. So on open ground the Boers were able to launch a heavy and prolonged attack on the exhausted Highland Brigade. The Scotsmen fought valiantly but were at a total disadvantage. Lord Carver's book *The Boer War* quotes from a letter by a Captain Foster written a week later: 'Last Monday week's fighting was too awful for anything and I shall never forget the sight of the Highland Brigade after their terrible slaughter. As they came streaming back towards our guns they were no longer men, they had no nerves, did not know where they were. We tried to rally them all the Monday but it was no good and some of the sights and things that happened I am glad to say that people in England do not know of.'[2] **Noel Seager**, a Brighton Grammar School boy, was serving in the Royal Army Medical Corps (RAMC) at the Base Hospital in Cape Town and wrote to say: 'We get some awful cases down from the front, but I think the worst were from Magersfontein. Some of the Black Watch had as many as seven bullet wounds.'

'Pals' regiments, where young men volunteered together from the same local area, were not constituted in the same way as in the Great War. However, records show that many pupils from grammar schools across the country volunteered for the war and the archivist at Brighton Grammar School has donated contemporary letters from their pupils who fought. Magersfontein was a terrible loss for a proud and professional regiment. Suffering over 900 casualties that day meant it was their worst defeat since 1798. The burden of losses from this battle fell heavily on the city of Dundee from where many recruits were drawn.

On 18 December 1899 the *Courier and Argus* newspaper from Dundee sported the headline: 'Black Watch Death Roll: Deplorable list of Casualties.' Clearly the returns then were far from complete. Then only forty-six were listed as killed, 160 wounded and 111 missing. The names of the casualties filled the front page each with poignant family details. For each of these men it was likely the only time they would ever be on the front of the newspaper.

- **Private J. McMillan**, aged thirty-eight, was a reservist reported missing. He lived in Walton St with his wife and two children. He had left the army but was recalled to serve in this war which was his first active service.
- **Sergeant T. Godfrey**, a native of Edinburgh, was also a reservist from the Black Watch. He was a doorkeeper at the Eastern club and a member of the Corps of Commissionaires, an agency that had been set up to provide employment for ex-soldiers. When he left for South Africa he had been engaged to be married.
- **Thomas Scullion** was also a reservist and had rejoined the regiment eighteen months previously. His death left behind a widow and three young children.
- The death of **Private J. Smith** was particularly affecting as his young wife's health had become increasingly delicate and soon after news of the battle reached home she herself had died. Private Smith's father lived locally.
- **Private Thomas Gowrie** was from Coupar Angus. He was in the reserves and had only a month to serve when he was called up. He had been appointed School Board officer and school instructor. Great sympathy was felt among all his classes for his mother, his young wife, brother and all his relatives who lived nearby.[3]

'It'll All Be Over by Christmas'

The *Daily Telegraph* newspaper set up a fund to help the families of those men who had died in these early battles of the war. The Shilling Fund for Our Soldiers' Widows and Orphans asked for a contribution of that amount from its contributors. Their front page was covered with a tragic litany of dead soldiers together with the number of their children.[4]

- **Private Kirkwood**, from Dunbar, a member of the Black Watch had four children. He died in Wynberg Hospital of wounds.
- **Private Grey** had four children and died at Magersfontein.

The loss of so many young men so early in a war that was deemed to be a certain victory for Britain would have been devastating. Whilst the press would have presented it as plucky young fighters for the Queen facing a setback, the tragedy for their families would have been immense. At this time in our social history army pensions were only for 'time served' soldiers who survived or a small gratuity just for the soldier's disability. These families would have to cope not just with their grief but an uncertain financial future. The Shilling Fund was established on an outpouring of sympathy. These charities, though well-meaning, could not cope with the avalanche of need as the war progressed. This will be explored in a later chapter.

Meanwhile **Fred Griffin**, a young security guard at Kimberley's diamond mines, was keeping a diary in the besieged town. Fred was a native of Devon who had lived with his family in a country cottage three miles from Honiton. Their farm had been in the family for three generations but like many rural properties it was rented, in this case from the Combe Estate. The long agricultural depression at the end of the nineteenth century forced many country dwellers from the land. Wages were low and sometimes part paid in cider. Many had already joined army regiments across the country attracted by a secure wage. In Devon this was particularly marked as witnessed by the names of some 400 men of the Devonshire regiment on the memorials in Exeter Cathedral. Within Fred's own family emigration had taken most of his siblings. In 1890 his sister Elizabeth had married her second cousin, a Devonian already farming in Nebraska, and moved to the United States to join him. Her brother John and his wife joined them in 1904. A cousin went to Canada and later still one of Fred's nieces had emigrated to Australia. Fred had chosen a different path but one which put him centre stage to the conflict in Kimberley.

In early November he was part of a unit travelling back to Kimberley with Captain Scott from an outpost at Vryburg, a hundred miles to the north. Kekewich, the military commander at Kimberley, had instructed his assistant Scott that there should be no surrender to the Boers but Scott feared for the local inhabitants with an approaching Boer army by whom they were heavily outgunned. The mayor had led a delegation to Scott asking for the town to be evacuated since the inhabitants feared for their lives. With all those things in mind Scott gave way and ordered the evacuation of the town.

On the very first night of the journey as everyone had laid down to rest there was a single shot which everyone had assumed to be a Boer attack. However, the shot was self-inflicted by Scott himself. Whether through fear of the repercussions, shame or both, Scott could not cope with his actions and ended his life with a single rifle shot to the head. Scott's death is recounted in Pakenham's book[5] but also by the young Fred Griffin to whom Scott had become a friend as well as a commander. He wrote: 'I felt it terribly because he talked to me about things previous, which was not the usual thing for an Officer to a private. He always took an interest in me and I felt I had lost the best friend I'd got. We wrapped him in a blanket and next morning took him about 10 miles further on and buried him near a store as he was, and there ended 21 years of Government Service.'

'It'll All Be Over by Christmas'

Losses on the battlefield were tragic but for Fred to lose his friend to a self-inflicted bullet must have cast a great shadow as he tried to come to terms with his feelings. After Scott's death he recounts how he travelled back to Kimberley not washing or changing his clothes for a week and always sleeping with a rifle by his side. He knew that the Boers had threatened to kill every 'rooinek' (a term used by the Boers to describe an English-speaking person). Fred arrived in Kimberley in the middle of November and we see day by day the anxiety as food dwindles in the town. The Boers had cut off their water supply but fortunately for them the engineers had been able to rig up a supply from the diamond mine. Fred gives a vivid description of the searchlights mounted on the pit-head of the mine constantly sweeping the countryside, illuminating any attacking Boers. The town was being constantly shelled but by mid-November the only casualties had been one human and several cats.

Rumour and counter-rumour would have swept through the population of the town and there was both fear and annoyance that the troops, who must have known of their state in the siege seemed to be doing little to help. They had no way of knowing of the difficulties the troops were facing in the surrounding countryside. Fred was aware that with good communications the people at home probably know more than them. 'We might as well be at the North Pole.' On 19 December he wrote: 'We've just heard of the brilliant British victory at Magersfontein.' According to Fred's entry the Boers were holed up in trenches whilst the British picked them off. The story was presumably spread to try and raise morale. With hindsight it seems an unfair deception.

The dwindling supplies of food and drink continued to be foremost in everyone's mind. On 5 December they had 'no good food' and had used up all the milk and beer the latter of which he said was 'deeply mourned'. By Christmas Day they had only mealie porridge, soup and bread.

The third of the major battles lost in the 'Black Week' of

December was at Colenso in eastern province of Natal. Fought on 15 December 1899, there were 1,138 British casualties. Here too, many young family men were lost. Records from the *Daily Telegraph*'s Shilling Charity Fund list a large number of men lost in the early months of the war. At Colenso they are from a variety of regiments and areas.[6]

- **Private Fugler** from the Cornish town of Launceston served in the Devonshire Regiment and left a widow and three children.
- **Private Joyce** from Dublin who served in the Royal Dublin Fusiliers and left a widow and one child.
- **Sergeant Hayes** was from Cork and served in the Royal Dublin Fusiliers. He left behind a widow and three children.
- **Private Murrask** from Chiswick was in the 2nd Battalion Royal West Surrey Regiment and left a widow and two children.
- **Corporal Pengelly** from Devonport of the 2nd Battalion Devonshire Regiment died that day leaving one child.

During the Boer War Ireland was still part of the British Empire and there were many Irish regiments. The country was a popular training ground for the British Army and the Curragh of Kildare west of Dublin was an army garrison. On the other hand, some Irish people supported the Boers, identifying with their anti-imperialist struggle against the British, and a few went to fight on their side.

Moses Mann was twenty-five years old and serving with the 2nd Battalion of the Devonshire Regiment. He was from Holne, a small, pretty village on the edge of Dartmoor. The 1891 census records him living with his widowed mother, his brother and sister and he is working as an agricultural labourer. We may surmise that, as with many agricultural labourers in Devon at the time, work was uncertain and poorly paid and Moses decided to choose a career in the army. In the spring quarter of 1899 he married Louisa Barnett in Totnes .Louisa was from a copper mining family in Tavistock but had been born in Scotland. By the 1891 census the family were back in Tavistock and Louisa, aged fifteen, was working as a servant. We can but imagine that, as with many working men, Louisa's father had been subject to the boom and bust of the mining industries which had meant the long move from Devon to Scotland and back.

For Moses and Louisa the South African war would not have been on the horizon at the time of their wedding and so it is to be hoped that they enjoyed a few summer months together before Moses was shipped to South Africa. He died on 17 December 1899, two days after what may have been his first battle at Colenso. Louisa was bereaved less than nine months after their marriage and we later find her as an in-patient and listed as a 'widow' at the East Cornwall and South Devon Hospital in Plymouth at the time of 1901 census.

George Ravenhill, a native of Birmingham who served with the Welsh Fusiliers was married with just one child, a daughter called Lilly, when the war started. He was the only private to win a Victoria Cross at Colenso. That VC was later taken from him as the result of being prosecuted for theft. By that time he had three children and was so penurious that they all ended up in the workhouse. His full story will be recounted later. Colenso also produced a tragedy for a family in the high command of the army. Freddie Roberts was the only son of Lord Roberts. At Colenso he was fighting under Buller's command and received his VC posthumously.

We are fortunate to have a first-hand account of the battle from **Mr Curnow**, a stretcher-bearer who hailed from Cornwall. He recalls that he had just joined the Natal Voluntary Ambulance Corps the week previously in Durban with 2,000 other men, and were then equipped and trained. The equipment consisted of waterproof sheets and blankets, cutlery, a haversack and water bottle. They were then trained to carry a stretcher, a new endeavour which he said took some practice but which he enjoyed once he had become competent in its use.

From there they took the train to a place called Frere in the province of Natal. This was to become one of the centres of medical help for the troops in those early days. Arriving about 8.30 in the morning they were told to sit and wait for a few hours and he describes how unbearable he found it under the hot sun. This unaccustomed heat in the South African sun was something that came as a shock to most British troops and he was relieved to move on to some shade in their camp.

It seems the troops were well aware of the impending battle at Colenso and on the following day, 14 December, he and his comrades heard several reports of the big guns seeming to come from the Colenso area. At the end of that day he says: 'thus ended the first day of N.V.A. and C in the Seat of War.' Clearly his phraseology implies they were on the edge of a momentous event and so they were. This young man from Cornwall was about to witness a level of violence unprecedented in his previous experience. On the 14th they took the long march towards Colenso and before the battle had even commenced they witnessed the wreckage of an armoured train. The British tried to protect the trains carrying troops with extra armour plating on the sides but this did not necessarily stop the Boers wrecking them by blocking the lines or derailment. This tactic was used quite frequently and, as Mr Curnow notes, resulted this time in the sad death of two young men. By the 15th he records:

> We were ordered to rest at the foot of a kopje [the Dutch word for small hill] on the top where officers of different ranks watching with keen interest the heavy battle that had not long commenced, occasionally there would be heavy firing which produced the sound like that of a waterfall and the Maxim Nordenfelt would be discharging its deadly weapon then come the big guns and during the whole of

that morning it seems that every weapon was being used with great vengeance. At 11 o'clock we sighted the Ambulance Wagons coming round the foot of the kopje and we ran to it for being a little anxious to know how the battle raged. We soon learnt the sad news which was that a reverse on our side would be the result of the Battle and we saw lots of wounded and learned that half the Dubs [Dublin Fusiliers] were being disarmed such as killed, wounded and taken prisoners. At 12 o'clock all hands were ordered to the top of the kopje and when in proper ranks we were marched onto the battle field where were soon put to work.

Recalling his first sight of the battle field he recalls:

When a boy I've often heard and seen beautiful pictures of war and its effects and at the same time, though it seems dreadful, yet have often possessed a liking of having just a birds eye view of a battlefield, at last it came and it was more than a birds eye view, more than I really expected. We were sent right onto the firing line such awful sight that I witnessed will ever be retained in my memory . . . the first sight we came to was 3 men who so it seems by the wounds were being killed by the Boer shrapnel.

Mr Curnow says that 1,100 were killed and wounded that day and that he witnessed the interment of Lord Roberts' son Freddie who was 'interred with military honours into the Colenso soil'. Mr Curnow provides a thoughtful reflection of everything he saw and did. He knows that his young self would have imagined this as exciting and glorious but the reality that confronted him and his comrades was far from that. This theme is reflected throughout in the comments of the soldiers. It is in sharp contrast to attitudes of glory on the battlefield engendered back home and woven into popular culture.

Sir Frederick Treves was based at the London Hospital in Whitechapel and was also surgeon to Queen Victoria, and is best known now for his involvement in the case of Joseph Merrick, the so-called 'Elephant Man'. He went out to South Africa arriving just before the Battle of Colenso. Setting the scene there just prior to the battle he describes the beauty of the far-off Drakensberg mountains as dawn rose. Then 'Before the peaks of the Drakensbergs were well alight the boom of our great guns sounded with startling clearness and it was evident that the prelude for our battle had begun.'[7] 'Our instructions were to proceed to Colenso and there to unload and camp. There was apparently no doubt that the village by the River Tugela would immediately be in our hands. Early rumours had it that the Boers had fled . . . These rumours were soon to be discredited by the incessant roar of cannon and later by the barking of the "pom pom" and the minor patter of rifle firing.' Just as in the false hopes about the Battle of Magersfontein given to people under siege in Kimberley this highly optimistic rumour was circulating around at Colenso.

Treves describes the aftermath of the battle:

When I arrived the ambulances were already coming in – the dreary ambulances each with a load of suffering, misery and death! Each waggon was drawn by ten mules and driven by a Kaffir [a derogatory term used to describe blacks at that time], and over the dusty hood of each the red cross flag waved in the shimmering heat. Each ambulance carried a certain number of wounded men who were well enough to sit up and a small number that were lying on stretchers 'the sitting down' and 'the lying down' cases as they were respectively called. Those who could move themselves were soon helped down from the wagon by willing hands, while the stretchers were taken out by relays of trained bearers. What a spectacle it was! Those were the very khaki clad soldiers who had, not so long ago left Waterloo [Station] spick and span amid a hurricane of cheers, and now they were coming back to camp silent and listless and scarcely recognisable as men. They were burnt a brown red by the sun, their faces covered in dust and sweat and in many cases blistered by the heat; their hands were begrimed, some were without tunics and the blue army shirts were stiff with blood. ... Their wounds were of all kinds and many had been shot in more places than one. Here was a man nursing a shattered arm in the blood stained rags of a torn up sleeve. There was another with his head bandaged up and his face painted with black streaks of dried blood holding a crushed helmet beneath his arm like a collapsible opera hat.

He described one man who was paralysed below the waist from a shot in the spine, repeatedly raising up his head so he could look at limbs which he could not move nor feel.

This disastrous battle was to be one of many fought to relieve the nearby town of Ladysmith. This town had been besieged on 30 October and troops under the command of General White had been driven back into the town to suffer similar privations to the town's residents. Just as in Kimberley, where people lived day-to-day hoping and praying for relief by British forces, here too a young man was keeping an account.

W. H. Heward was a railway worker in Ladysmith and his diary starts in early December. He talks of turning up at the station every day for roll call. At that early stage they are getting 12 ounces of meat every day and a little tea, coffee and sugar. The meat ration sounds fairly generous initially but he wrote that it often smelt bad and 'the best stuff is commandeered by the military or shopkeepers who keep their prices high'. Prices were an issue throughout the siege.[8] He has some wry observations about the army officers holed up with the troops. 'They [the officers] are an overbearing lot of men – I certainly wouldn't stick being a Tommy with such men over me.' We will see a suppressed anger at the behaviour of the officer class repeated in other accounts from ordinary soldiers.

Ladysmith was a difficult town to defend. One contemporary account describes it like an open tea cup with the side partly blown off. Boer shells landed regularly in the town and Mr Heward gives us a graphic description of this: 'One poor fellow had an arm blown off and a dog was seen running away with it.'

He saw that the men who'd been out on the hills and had had to drink muddy water were being violently sick. The illness was enteric fever and it was to be the greatest killer in this war. By Christmas the rations had shrank to 'only bread and soup and now Mr Spencer's cows have been commandeered the milk has gone'. It is a reminder that this was still a rural setting. It is hoped that the soldiers who took the cows knew how to milk them!

Already feelings of sorrow and loss were beginning to be expressed in poetry. Lance Sergeant W. Staton of the York and Lancashire regiment had left York on 13 December 1899 and sailed from Liverpool arriving eventually in Durban on New Year's Eve. In this time he would have heard about the disasters of 'Black Week' and more was to follow when he experienced the Battle at Spion Kop. In his diary is this unattributed poem.

<u>Bereaved Mothers</u>
He went away with the soldiers
My child my only son;
I saw him pass the window
In the glow of the autumn sun
I could pick him out from
Amongst them
My boy with his smiling face
The upward look of his kindly eyes
And his careless boyish grace

'It'll All Be Over by Christmas'

I got the paper this morning
And hastily glanced it o'er
While a chill came over me creeping
That I had never felt before
A warning of what was coming
A voice that would not be stilled.
I looked at the missing and wounded
And he was among the killed.

Did he die alone, I wonder why,
Was there no one near my soldier boy
When he passed to the great unseen?
Could I only see him once again,
(Though he only came home to die)
To kiss that face I love so well
And whisper a last good bye.
You boast of the glory of battle
You join in a country's cheers
Have you thought of the many widows?
Have you thought of the orphan's tears?
There is many a desolate mother
In the breadth of our land today
That weeps in hopeless sorrow
For her dead so far away

Our Father in heaven hear us,
And answer us while we pray
And in mercy and the Battle
That our country is in today
To many be a soldier's honour
To die at his country's call
But it's hard to remember the glory
When our women have lost our all.[9]

The only anthology of Boer War poetry has been out of print since 1978. However, poems written by Thomas Hardy, such as 'Drummer Hodge', can be found in other collections. Anonymous poems like this one and a later one by James Homeyard were written with great feeling about the effects of the war on families and reflect the direct experience of those bereaved. They contrast markedly with those written to stir patriotic feelings about the war usually by those at home with no direct experience.

Chapter 3

THE CALL FOR VOLUNTEERS AND THE BESIEGED TOWNS

By Christmas 1899, far from celebrating a victory, the British realised that if they did not pour more troops into the war victory could not be assured. Suing for peace with the Boers and losing strategic influence over the gold in the Rand was, however, out of the question.

In the War Office that Christmas frantic plans were put into operation to raise a volunteer force. So while Fred Griffin and Mr Heward were having a miserable Christmas with their meagre rations, the English high command, though well fed, were not enjoying the season either. Their tables in London would no doubt be replete with goose and plum pudding, a feast which would have satisfied the residents of Kimberley and Ladysmith, but the generals were preoccupied with the raising an army to stave off defeat in the war and their meals would have been taken for granted.

The first tranche of recruitment to what became known as the Imperial Yeomanry was largely amongst middle- and upper-class men aged twenty to thirty-five. Preference was given to unmarried men or widowers without children. Perhaps the powers that be realised how many children had already been orphaned by the conflict. They were to be of good character; expected height was 5ft 3in although the City of London demanded 5ft 4in; chest measurement was to be 34in and weight 115lbs. These requirements for largely middle-class recruits demonstrate how much smaller people were then. They had to convince the colonel of the unit they were to join that they were good marksmen and accomplished riders. Each was expected to have his own horse and to dress in a Norfolk jacket. It is hard to see why a woollen jacket, hot in the sun and absorbent in the rain, was seen to be a suitable item of clothing for the South African climate but it seems that what was seen as proper in England must be right for South Africa. Recruits were stirred by patriotism and a desire for glory in the war.[1]

One recruit to the Imperial Yeomanry was **Percy Hobbs** from Portsmouth. Percy was from a naval family, born in Plymouth but the family had transferred to Portsmouth through the father's job as a torpedo instructor. He was a dapper young man, photographed before he left for the war in a jacket and straw boater. At recruitment he was 5ft 9½in tall and weighed just 127lbs. This weight was similar to that of most young men who were recruited at the time. He trained for thirty days and left for South Africa on 22 February 1900. We know little of his time in South Africa but the active recruitment at this time indicates that the army needed constant replacements.

Records at the National Archives show a variety of previous occupations for men who joined the 29th, 30th, 31st and 49th Companies of the Imperial Yeomanry. **H. Pierce** was a traveller, **J. L. Lyons** a huntsman, **W. V. Williams, H. Ferguson** and **E. J. Edwards** were clerks, **J. Williams** a grocer, **W. Bache** a fitter, **B. B. Bedford** a horse dealer, **J. Hayes** an engineer, **F. J. Cowena** a dentist and **J. Riley** a butcher. No doubt the huntsman, horse dealer and engineer would have skills to offer in the war but the extremes of the veldt would have come hard to those who were used to sitting at a desk. The dentist, too would have been welcome since some recruits had such poor teeth that they could not eat the hard biscuits that constituted the staple diet of the 'Tommies' or ordinary British soldier.

It was not just volunteers for the Yeomanry that were intended

The Call for Volunteers and the Besieged Towns

to swell the ranks of those British troops going to South Africa. **Thomas Galley**, who joined the Worcestershire Regiment, recounts how he was recruited. Thomas was eighteen and he and his sister were living with their aunt and uncle since their parents had died. He had a job working in a carpet factory with his uncle but in his diary said that the work did not suit him. So he set out one morning to offer himself to the local regiment. A desire for adventure and the patriotic fervour which surrounded the early part of the war impelled many young men to join up.

Once inducted into a new battalion of the Worcestershire Regiment they were sent on a recruiting march starting in Evesham and ending in Dudley. Passing through such towns as Pershore, Stourbridge and Kidderminster, they had taken on 200 recruits by the end. The sight of young soldiers in dress uniform whipping up support for Queen and Country would have stirred up patriotic feelings. Other carpet factories would have lost their young workers and for those without work it would have been an immediate draw. We will see that the following year a second tranche of the Yeomanry was rather different. As the high command of the army became desperate for recruits, more men from poorer backgrounds were recruited. They were attracted as much by the money as by patriotic feelings. The bar to married men with children was lifted. Their training was poor and the state of their health meant that 700 had to be shipped home as unfit to fight. This demonstrated the poor state of health of many working-class men at this time and it was this that eventually influenced social legislation during the 1900s aimed to remedy this.

Fred Griffin, in Kimberley, knew of the raising of the Imperial Yeomanry and wondered if any of his friends at home would volunteer. His experiences with the heat caused him to muse that Australians would be better suited to join the fight. He says that by New Year's Day the Army Service Corps had taken over the food supply and on that day a woman was killed near the meat market while trying to get some milk. The same day they had received seasonal messages by heliograph all the way from Ladysmith and from Governor Milner. It is interesting to see that some communication worked surprisingly well. His feelings go out to the civilians: 'I wonder how well the women and children take this abominable siege.' A little later he refers to his friend, Sam Northcote, who is very ill and weak. Sam is a married man with a young child and Fred comments 'But the youngster seems strong and healthy.' He calls on them to try and keep their spirits up. It's not long until the tables are turned and in early February Fred is hospitalised with dysentery. In the first two days the stomach pains are very bad but he appreciated the nurses who looked after them. Clearly Northcote has recovered because he returned the compliment and visited Fred each of the twelve days he's there. Fred had to leave before he was fully recovered because other people needed the beds. When he left the medics allowed him a tin of golden syrup; whether this is an aid to recovery or simply a treat to cheer him up he doesn't say.

After this the shelling continued and the food had virtually run out but finally on 16 February 1900 Kimberley was relieved by a force lead by General French. His relief is palpable but probably like anyone subject to prolonged hunger his first thought is of food: 'We now get extra meat but luxuries such as butter and jam have to be bought'. It seems his enthusiasm for South Africa has not been dampened by his experiences since, once the siege is lifted, he writes to his mother: 'I wonder what has been going on at home. Remember me to some of my friends. Tell them this is the coming field for emigration. Did you buy those shares I advised you of?' Fred saw his future in South Africa.

Robert Slattery was another working-class lad who joined up at the age of 18. Being a Lancashire boy he opted for the Loyal North Lancashire Regiment. Robert had an unusually troubled childhood and we can only guess that this may have been a factor in a career that would help him escape from those painful memories. As a child his parents had fought frequently and he

The Call for Volunteers and the Besieged Towns

had to contend with the drinking of his father, Daniel, which seems to have been a major factor. Prior to the final quarrel his mother, Mary, had been unwell. That night they argued and Daniel pushed her over. The neighbour who gave evidence at the inquest was called that night but a doctor wasn't and Mary died a few days later. The inquest achieved full prominence in the *Liverpool Mercury*, finding death by natural causes accelerated by gross neglect and violence. The father was discharged but clearly did not want to stick around.

Robert and his two siblings were taken in by a paternal aunt in Accrington and it was here he found his first job in a small factory printing patterns on calico and other materials. The following year he joined up and after some years in Ceylon he went to South Africa six months before the outbreak of conflict. He would have been one of the 10,662 men who were already in the country. His earliest taste of fighting was at the siege of Kimberley. He describes being shelled incessantly throughout that time. In a letter to his old boss in Accrington he reveals that soldiers too suffered the same privations as the inhabitants of the town living on horse flesh and mealies. He said: 'It came awful hard to us that after 2 months siege we were nearly always hungry, some of our fellows used to catch frogs and eat them but I couldn't go them at all.'

He was later involved in a number of marches and sorties and from this one can begin to comprehend the distances that the soldiers had to travel. One duty involved escorting the Boer General Cronje down to Cape Town from the northern regions, a trip of perhaps a thousand miles. Cronje was captured at the Battle of Paardeberg in late February 1900. It was the first overwhelming victory for the British since the disasters in December 1899 but for Cronje it was a double humiliation since his fellow Boers ostracised him for what they considered his disastrous tactics which lost them the battle. Eventually Cronje exiled himself to the United States of America, never to return.

Robert was one of those who took part in the capture of the Boers' capital of Pretoria on 6 June. Boer towns were not cities like those in Britain and this must have come as a surprise to the British troops. Robert's description of Pretoria was that 'It was not much of a place.'

The ongoing campaign to relieve Ladysmith involved a number of fierce battles in the surrounding countryside. Before it was finally relieved, on 28 February, 3,196 had died and a further 1,457 were wounded.

At this stage those who fought and died were still the regular army assisted by sailors from the Royal Navy. The volunteer force, the Imperial Yeomanry, was still being recruited and trained back in Britain. On 6 January, at Wagon Hill, a fierce battle erupted at night. Whilst the naval guns were being hauled into position at the top of the hill ready for combat there was a sudden volley of shots from the Boers. Taken by surprise and in pitch darkness the British knocked over the lanterns and ran in a panic to try and find their rifles. A chaotic scene ensued. The difficulties were exacerbated by the fact that the young British soldiers were wearing the same 'slouch' hats as their Boer opponents and confusion reigned. Battle raged for hours. The terrible tally was seventeen officers and 158 men killed, and twenty-eight officers and 221 men wounded. The Devonshire Regiment bore the brunt, losing all but one of their officers.

One casualty of this battle was **Charles Webber**, a regular soldier from Barnstaple in Devon. His knee was smashed by an explosive bullet and his leg had to be amputated well above the knee. That was in January and by October he was back home and his case featured in two local newspapers, the *Totnes Times* and the *Exeter Gazette*, which protested at the level of payment the War Office had offered him.

Sergeant **James Boseley** had Irish parentage on his mother's side. Showing the strong links the military had in Ireland, his father Private Charles Boseley married Ellen Power in Tipperary in 1868. James was the oldest and was born in Kamptee, India, in 1873 where his father was posted. Later the family returned to England, settling at Maidstone in Kent, where Charles worked as an agricultural labourer until his death in 1883. James was sent the Royal Hibernian Military School and subsequently enlisted in the British army in Londonderry aged sixteen in 1889. As a sergeant in the Royal Artillery, he was at the Battle of Wagon Hill where he was hit by a 95lb shell. His left arm and leg were shattered and subsequently both limbs on his left side had to be amputated. His survival from these terrible injuries was nothing short of a miracle.

Hard on the heels of Wagon Hill came the Battle of Venterspruit. Private **John Welsford** died here, leaving a wife and three children. John was from Bideford in North Devon and worked in that area as a printer but by the age of twenty he had joined up and was living in an army encampment near Pembroke in Wales. Of his three children, the first, Annie was born to his young wife, Sarah, in Wales. After her death he married Clara from his native Bideford and they had Ada and Richard who was born after John's death.

Probably the most catastrophic battle of the war took place just four days after Venterspruit on a hill called Spion Kop, 'Spy Hill' in Afrikaans. It is said that more men died here, at the top of this hill and in such a small area of land, than in any other battle at any time in history anywhere in the world. So many of the British soldiers who died were from the cold, wet climes of northern England. After the battle, difficulty of access to the hill had meant leaving wounded men far too long without water and their suffering must have been terrible. The Acre of Massacre, where bodies were piled and buried as they fell remains as a monument to that terrible day. In this war the misunderstanding about the safety of reaching the summit of an African hill or kop seemed to recur, endangering the lives of so many. Spion Kop was strategically placed en route to the town of Ladysmith. If only the British could have taken it this would have constituted a major milestone in freeing the besieged town.

General Buller, previously in commander at Colenso, commanded the troops that day but other officers played a major part. Amongst them was **Lieutenant-Colonel Alexander Thorneycroft** leading his own unit of mounted infantry. He was a towering figure of a man and a confident soldier .He set out to sketch the hill the day before the battle. Unfortunately this sketch was not accurate; his estimate of where the summit was fell far short of the reality. This, combined with the inability to take sufficient water to the top, proved fatal to the young soldiers climbing the hill that early morning. The Boers were waiting for them on a neighbouring hill which was crucially higher than the British position. As the troops gingerly raised their heads from their shallow trenches at dawn the Boer rifles easily picked them off. Many died with a single shot through the left temple as they turned their heads instinctively away from the fierce glare of the rising African sun.

The heat of the sun was intense, easily reaching 38 degrees Centigrade throughout the day. Lack of water exacerbated problems and for young men used to the cool wet climes of Lancashire the situation would have been intolerable. Identity tags were routinely sewn into soldiers' jackets to aide identification. However, in the searing heat these were discarded and thus many bodies remained unidentified following this carnage. The deaths of injured men were hastened by lying in the hot sun without water. The famous photo of British soldiers dead in the trench shown on the front cover was in fact taken on 26 January 1900. Many soldiers, of course, had died immediately but the difficulty of getting to the top of that precipitous hill to try and tend to men must have led to many more casualties. A first-hand account from Mr Curnow the stretcher-bearer states that 'at the top we went and were presented with a horrible sight – lots of

The Call for Volunteers and the Besieged Towns

dead and wounded were scattered like dead animals'. He continues:

> While there and attending one wounded man which we managed to get onto the stretcher about four Boers gathered round us and conversed in English with one of our chaps, while their two guns were fired by the Boers at our men and was soon responded a fear took hold of us, soon we made track to descend a very difficult hill to get down after labouring hard we managed to reach the vans and then rested ourselves. Unfortunately we found after a while that the vans were all full necessitating us to take them to the field hospital. When we reached there we were ordered to the pontoon bridge. So after a little rest and beef tea which our wounded received from the attendants we were on the march under a boiling sun. About fifty men were being conveyed to the same place.

Albert Collet's diary describes how he went to relieve the Lancashire Fusiliers.

> We got there and what should we hear but that deadly sound of the Pom pom and all at once the shells burst over our heads and there were a lot of dead men lying all over the hill than when we had been up there – a shell came over and killed two men and wounded four and the two it killed their clothes caught and smouldered and burnt them unrecognisable and one of the men ran to take the ammunition from them and one of the officers shouted out that you can't do any good as the poor fellows are dead. Such a thing I had never seen in my life before and don't wish to see another such horrible day like that again, poor fellows.[2]

It is extraordinary to note that two major figures of the twentieth century were present that day. Winston Churchill, then just twenty-five. who had previously been a prisoner of the Boers, was working as a reporter for the London *Morning Post*. Mahatma Gandhi was serving as a stretcher-bearer in the Natal Indian Ambulance Corps. Churchill wrote: 'Corpses lay here and there. Many of the wounds were of a horrible nature. The shallow trenches were choked with dead and wounded.' Foreshadowing the horrors of modern warfare he described, 'Massive clouds of orange light . . . men being blown to atoms.' The dead bodies piled high in the shallow trenches were horror enough but bodies that were simply blown out of existence added a new dimension to this terrible conflict.[3] It is said that what Gandhi witnessed that day influenced his later total commitment to pacifism.

James Candy was born on 27 December 1868. In 1887 he joined the South Lancashires in Liverpool at the age of eighteen. By 1894 he was posted to Egypt and whilst there had married a Mary Elizabeth Bailey and in September 1894 she gave birth to a daughter whose birth was registered at Cairo. James was posted to India soon afterwards and sadly his wife died there. Left alone with his young daughter, James returned home to Lancashire and by 1895 was working as a blacksmith at Albion Mills, Blackburn. James was a Wesleyan, active in promoting religion, a passion he carried to the end of his life and continued preaching whilst serving in the South African War.

In 1896 he married again, this time to Elizabeth Alice Haworth from Darwen and two daughters followed soon afterwards, Martha Alice in 1897 and Bertha in 1898. As an army reservist, James was called up to serve in the Boer War. Promoted to sergeant he went to South Africa with the South Lancashires. He wrote to his wife two days after arriving:

Estcourt, Christmas Day. We landed at Durban on 23rd December and entrained same evening travelling all night

The Call for Volunteers and the Besieged Towns

and arrived here yesterday at twelve noon, Christmas Eve. The people in Durban gave us a good send-off but it was a wearisome journey up country. We got some tea and bread and butter during the night and we had a further tuck of bread, cheese and coffee at Mooi River at nine in the morning. We are now about 8 miles from the Boar [sic] position so we may get into action any moment. I came out this morning with twelve men to guard a bridge at the entrance to the town. We all stop here until tomorrow morning. The weather is hot and rather trying after England. We are under canvas and the food is pretty good though rough and ready. There is plenty of beef as our men have brought in 3,000 head of cattle and horses belonging to the Boers. There are about 8,000 troops here and a few thousand down at Mooi River. Of course Buller's Army is in front about six or seven miles away. It is half past one, dinner time and I am sitting under out of the sun and thinking how differently I should have spent Christmas at home. We have had nothing to eat since five this morning and I don't know what time we shall get it – I'm afraid it will be but a poor Christmas dinner. We hope to relieve Ladysmith shortly. We are getting the Lancashire brigade up; the Fusiliers arrived same day as ourselves. I suppose there will be some Darwen lads amongst them but I don't happen to know them.

The war wasn't over by Christmas and the soldiers were facing the uncertainty about food that would dog them throughout this war. The idea that Ladysmith would soon be relieved echoes the hopes of our siege diarists, Fred Griffin in Kimberley and Mr Heward in Ladysmith itself. Later there was much criticism of the British military tactics that allowed these sieges to drag on but for the people involved there was just the desperate wish to get it over and done with and for the soldier the desire to get on with the job.

James Candy wrote again to his wife on 22 January just two days before the battle at Spion Kop. 'Kiss the children for their dada and tell them we will have a Christmas day and a week at Blackpool, God willing, when Dada comes home. If I can I will bring something home for them and you.' Those wishes were never fulfilled as James died that terrible day on Spion Kop, under General Warren's command.[4] The bitter irony is that just four days later James would have finished his time as a reservist and been able to be discharged. Just as with **John Welsford's** death another widow was left with three young children to support.

Henry Raven was twenty-one years old and was wounded at Spion Kop. He died some five months later of enteric in Newcastle, South Africa. When Henry joined the Lancashire Fusiliers as a band boy aged fourteen in 1891 he said that he did know where he came from. We do know that by 1897 he had married Catherine at St Luke's Church in Preston, the base for the Lancashire Fusiliers. Catherine was born in Aldershot so we presume she herself was of a military family. In 1898 their baby daughter Emily was born and the following year Henry was called up to fight in South Africa. It is likely that Henry, like James Candy, left from Lancashire mid-December Christmas 1899. It would have been the last time Catherine and Emily saw him.

Charles Webber's case illustrated the kind of catastrophic injuries that dum dum bullets could cause. At Spion Kop there were more of such gross injuries. The cemetery at Spearman's farm shows that some survived the battle only to die of wounds within the following week. This was despite the efforts of a dedicated medical team led by Sir Frederick Treves, the Queen's surgeon who had been at Colenso. In his diary Treves gives us just one such example:

> I remember at Chievely one morning before breakfast watching a solitary man approach the hospital lines. He was as melancholy an object as ever a war has produced. He was

The Call for Volunteers and the Besieged Towns

a soldier who had fought at Colenso, at Vaal Krantz and before Pieters, and he was now staggering towards the hospital, a ragged, broken down, khaki coloured spectre of a man. He dragged his rifle with him; his belt was gone; his helmet was poised at the back of his head; his frowsy tunic was thrown over his shoulders; he was literally black with flies. His clothes had not been off for many days. He had missed the ambulance, he said, and had walked to the hospital. How far he had come he could not tell, nor could anyone gather how he fared or how he had slept. All that was evident was that he was wet with dew and had spent the night in the open. He knew that for vague hours he had been making his way with ever faltering steps and failing eyes towards the red cross flag on the crest of the hill. Now he had reached it, he said that he had a touch of dysentery and was about played out.

Poor lad! This was a sorry homecoming at the last. A squalid ending of a march; shuffling in alone without a single comrade with no fifes and drums, no cheering crowd and no proud adoration of mother or wife. He was helped to a bell tent and put to bed on a stretcher and on the stretcher he died and this was the end of his soldiering. Sic transit Gloria mundi.[5]

One man catastrophically injured that day undoubtedly owed his life to Treves's skill. **Patrick Kelly** had been laid on a stretcher and deemed unlikely to survive when Treves found him. He had been up on the kop for two days amongst the dead and dying crawling around trying to find the water bottles of dead soldiers. Treves performed an operation that amputated both his arms and collar bones. He praised Kelly's absolute bravery since this surgery was performed without anaesthetic.

It seems impossible to us now that men so grossly incapacitated could have survived such traumas 115 years ago.

However, we do have a first-hand account from Sir Frederick Treves who operated on Patrick Kelly in the field hospital. He says he was the bravest patient he'd ever had, bearing all the pain with dignity and that he only became upset when he thought they had lost the bottle of beer donated to him. Both Boseley and Kelly were feted on their return home to Britain and we will see in a later chapter how they were affected in civilian life.

Other wounded men made it home but sought treatment in this country. **William Ward** of the King's Royal Rifle Corps was twenty-nine years old and had been wounded at Spion Kop.[6] He had been hit by a bullet in front of his right thigh, another in the left forearm and there was a piece of shell lodged in the back of his left hand. He had been operated on in Pietermaritzburg and there were two scars leading to the bone dying. The forearm was stiffened and muscles wasted and was at an angle to the upper arm. The wrist was almost immobile and his fingers totally stiff. X-rays showed small bits of shell in front of the elbow and other pieces around the middle of the forearm. This level of incapacity would severely restrict his work prospects.

The Salvation Army sent personnel to South Africa early in the war to offer spiritual comfort to the soldiers. Captain Mary Murray wrote an account in a book entitled *All the World* published in 1901.[7] She writes graphically of the soldiers' lives and she evinces sympathy for the Boers as well. Thus we obtain a more rounded view of life in the middle of this terrible conflict. Early on she is at Pietermaritzburg Hospital and recounts that she is not seeing wounded but the 'far sadder sight of wards crowded with men suffering rheumatism and dysentery'. These 'young men who a few months or even a few weeks ago were full of life and strength are now prematurely old; their rheumatism coming from having slept all night on a damp floor and being soaked through.' Religious meetings were, of course, arranged but as ever the Salvation Army acted in a welfare role; writing letters home for soldiers too weak to manage this themselves and increasingly

The Call for Volunteers and the Besieged Towns

responding to communications from worried relatives back home.

Despite being a non-combatant she braved some terrible sights. After Spion Kop she had also travelled through the Boer trenches and witnessed the aftermath of women's involvement in the conflict. 'Several women have been found dead in the trenches with bandoliers on. The most pitiful sight was a woman dying whilst trying to look after her tiny baby. No one had been relieved for days, the dying and the dead were lying side by side.'

Mary Murray recounts tending to British soldiers after the battle. 'The first man I helped to the hospital was shot through the arm and the shoulder. He presented a truly pitiful appearance struggling against a sharp hailstorm stained with blood . . . "It wasn't these scratches I mind," he gasped as we stopped to take breath after having been blown round a corner. "But that my mates have been shot down like dogs. Eight hours we have lain to be shot at".' Despite the devastation, she observed that the night after the battle of Spion Kop there were only two army nurses and one civilian there to tend to 700 wounded.

Thomas Stones from Blackburn was with the 2nd Battalion of the Lancashire Fusiliers. Preston Archives keeps letters written to him from his sister, brother-in-law and other residents of the town throughout the war. Sadly Thomas's letters have not survived but their replies reflect Thomas's experiences and give valuable descriptions of life back home. Thomas was fortunate to have survived the slaughter at Spion Kop and Jimmy, his brother in law, tells him how everyday they scan the *Daily Mail* for casualty lists. There would be many other relatives who would be anxiously doing the same. Jimmy had recounted how there had been a big do in Preston the previous November with 1,200 men leaving for the front. Maybe James Candy, Henry Raven and John Welsford had been amongst that contingent. The letters must have provided Thomas with some light-hearted enjoyment about friends at home. One such friend gives news of who's going out together and what marriages are planned. A little later Deborah jokes with her brother that he has been away so long that he will end up marrying a Boer girl! Deborah and Jimmy run a pub called the 'Stop and Rest Inn' and she jokes with her brother that perhaps he should leave all his possessions to the 'inebriates home'.

Even after the slaughter at Wagon Hill, Venterspruit and Spion Kop, the town of Ladysmith had not been relieved and the frustration of its inhabitants was the same as for those in Kimberley. Mr Heward noted that 'There are one hundred and ten thousand English troops, why are they letting us be cooped up like this?' By the end of 1899 he himself had lost over a stone in weight through diarrhoea and he notes that fifty men were going to hospital every day.

In a characteristically graphic description he tells us that the body of one his fellow railway guards, who had died of enteric, was cut in half by a shell as it lay in the town hall. An unexploded Boer shell was dug up by two of the naval men who hammered at it causing it to explode, blowing off one man's leg and another's stomach. Neither, he said, were expected to live.

With other food running out the horses were slaughtered for meat. Showing the kind of gallows humour which is helpful in such situations, they made their own form of the popular hot drink of Bovril and called it 'Chevril', from the French for horse. Mr Heward reported that a 'Kaffir boy' had said that if they were given horse instead of beef with their mealie they would stop working. He remarks wryly 'That will be serious as they are the only ones who do any work round there.' This noteworthy acknowledgement of the contribution that black people is unusual. **Trooper Fielding** from Darwen in Lancashire said there were only 100 horses left as they had eaten the rest and they looked like 'hat racks with their ribs sticking out'. 'But alas and a lack where are our gee gees? We trained them, we groomed them, we rode them, we fed them and then to wind things up we made a meal of them!' (from Blackburn District Libraries newspaper cutting).

The Call for Volunteers and the Besieged Towns

Charles Henry Ruddock walked all the way from Radstock in Somerset aged just 13 years old to find himself a job at the goods' yard in Birmingham and then aged just 15 or 16 enlisted with the Staffordshire Regiment. After service in Malta, Egypt and Gibraltar he was sent to South Africa in 1899. At the siege of Ladysmith he and his comrades were starving. To assuage their hunger they were willing to eat anything and when they found raw barley it was consumed without thinking. Unfortunately it fermented in their stomachs and some men died as a result. His group were dubbed the 'Ragged Hundred', a soubriquet describing their conditions.

Arthur Wilson of the Scots Greys arrived in Kimberley on 14 February 1900, the day it was relieved, and gives an interesting account:

> I was scouting in advance with my Troop this day and was one of the first in Kimberley. We rode over the famous Blue grounds where the ore is laid out for exposure to the sun, a process by which the diamonds are extracted. We had been very short of food, we only had one pound of biscuits about four per man, with a little tea and sugar when we left Modder River. We had oats in one wallet and ammunition in the other, hay nets slung across our saddles. We lost an awful lot of horses on this ride, heat and exhaustion being the trouble. Thirst also played us all up and what water we did get was as black as ink and vile but still it was a drink.

Eventually, on 28 February 1900 Ladysmith was relieved and people of the town went wild with joy. Women rushed towards the relieving British troops kissing the horses and the soldiers equally. Everyone ran through the street shouting with joy and the usual divisions between races was set aside for that one day. Off-duty soldiers, officers, townsfolk, Zulus and dhoolie bearers all lined the pavements to watch as the relieving troops, led by General Buller, came riding into the town.

After the euphoria had subsided the sentiments of the ordinary soldiers were a little different. **F. Bennet**, of the 1st Rifle Brigade, wrote home to his brother, Charlie, in Plymouth, after Ladysmith was eventually relieved. 'I'm having a well-earned rest after the hard work that had to be done to relieve Ladysmith. I can tell you Charlie words cannot describe what was seen and endured by all the troops under General Buller what with charging hills and storming trenches we had a very lively time of it.' Their mother had written to say that Charlie was thinking of volunteering. However, his brother in South Africa advises: 'I think it shows a splendid spirit on the part of all those who have volunteered yet my advice is stay where you are. We had not tents, blankets or coats from January 9th till after Ladysmith was relieved. It rained every night as regular as clockwork .I wonder how it is I feel as well as I do now.' He jokes that it may be 'lack of whisky'.[8]

Despite all the horror and exhaustion of the battles there was a desire to maintain a sense of normality and discussion of their favourite football teams seemed a good way to achieve this. In his diary 'At the Front', **Mick Gallagher** from Liverpool recorded 'We heard today that Buller lost a thousand men and that Southampton and Aston Villa were in for the final of the cup. The things that might have been! I'll see the cup in Liverpool yet!'[9] This might sound callous but from a man who had previously talked about sleeping rough on the veldt, travelling with sick men who had no doctor and being stopped from getting milk by their officer, the need for some light entertainment was palpable. He also gives an insight into the vagaries of their pay saying that when they signed articles to enlist they were to be paid 1 shilling and 9 pence a day but it was discovered once they were on their way to South Africa that this was a mistake and that in reality their pay was only 1 shilling and 3 pence.

Football was a major diversion for working-class men at this

The Call for Volunteers and the Besieged Towns

time and is mentioned by other soldiers. **Reuben Evans** wrote a diary giving a comprehensive account of his part in the war. Together with this diary was a satirical account of the war told in the style of a football match.

> The South African Game – Empire v Transvaal
> The teams were made up of the top generals from both sides. For the Empire it was Roberts in goal; Baden-Powell and White, full backs; Hunter, Kitchener and Dundonald as half backs; Buller and Clery, right wing; French centre forward; Methuen and Kelly-Kenny on the left wing.
>
> For the Transvaal and Orange Free State, Kruger was in goal; Cronje and Steyn, full backs; Botha, Prinsloo and Oliver, full backs; De Wet and Viljoen right wing; Joubert centre forward; Jinyman and Villebois on the left wing.
>
> The referee was Public Opinion and the kick off was 11th October 1899, the day, of course, the war began.
>
> The match was the attraction of the season and was played on the home team's ground in South Africa. The last time the two teams met was in 1881 and ended in a very unsatisfactory manner. This time the visitors brought over 20,000 supporters and were without doubt a team that anyone would be proud of. The home team won the toss for choice of grounds and Joubert kicked off. They at once became aggressive and were becoming dangerously near the visitors' goal. But White at the back was playing a sound game and repelled attack after attack when the home team seemed bound to score; in fact the visitors' backs B.P. and White were playing grandly and although the home forwards were in the visitors' territory they failed to score.
>
> The Empire's forwards now began to get into their stride, and French working like a machine round his opponent completely beat Cronje and with a swift lightning shot he found the net with a beauty (Kimberley). Soon after

this goal, Cronje was dismissed from the field (Paardeberg) thus weakening the home defence.

Buller who all along had been playing a steady game and was now seen to advantage and although being stopped several times in his grand rushes he came back again and again and shattering his opponents' defence he came dashing on and by a superhuman effort, entirely on his own scored a grand goal (Ladysmith). Soon after the home team lost the services of their best player, Joubert.

A strong wind was now blowing across the field thus giving the left wing of the visitors a chance to show their paces. Kelly-Kenny and French were now very prominent with some splendid work and were passing beautifully. The home team repeatedly tried to stop the grand combination but all their efforts proved futile. Kelly-Kenny now transferred to French and that famous player showed his sterling qualities by scoring another (Bloemfontein). The play was now in the home team's territory and the visitors' forwards were pressing when the whistle blew for half time with the score British Empire 3, Transvaal and Orange Free State 0.

The teams now appeared on the field to contest the second half of the game. The home team supporters were in despair for they saw that bar accidents their pets would lose the game. The visitors were playing with a confidence that was a treat to see while the home team resorted to dirty tricks (abusing the white flag). Try how they would the home team could not stem the pressure the visitors' forwards put into the game. French again got possession and tricking the half backs promptly made the game secure by scoring another fine goal (Johannesburg). Baden-Powell, the mainstay of the Empire's defence was now transferred to the front rank. His heroic defence, had been the admiration of all and he completely demonstrated to the spectators that he could play forward as well as back.

The Call for Volunteers and the Besieged Towns

Some very fast play was now seen, the ball travelling with lightening velocity towards the goal. The visitors made a grand combined rush and after some splendid play in front of the goal the ball was sent into the goal amidst cheers of thousands (Pretoria). The home team was completely staggered and Kruger their goal keeper left his net at the mercy of his opponents. The home team contended that the goal was off side but the referee ruled otherwise. The whistle now blew for time; the score being, after a hard fought game, British Empire 5, Transvaal and Orange Free State 0.

W. H. Francis from Folkestone was twenty-one years old when he joined the East Kent Regiment and sailed for South Africa. He wrote a diary which has been lovingly transcribed by his great-granddaughter, Melanie, for a school project to which she has added her own research about the war.

They had already heard the good news concerning the Relief of Ladysmith on the boat travelling to South Africa. They disembarked at Cape Town and. travelled on by train to Naauypoort. He records that two men were tried and shot for selling fodder and at the same time two Boer prisoners were also tried. No explanation is given for this but his great granddaughter remarks that these impromptu courts seemed to be a feature of this war, imposing summary punishments. This would tie in with a story given to me in person by **Mrs Attrill**, a lady over ninety years old. She told me that her father, who fought in South Africa, was made, with others, to witness a British soldier hanged for desertion. Well over 100 years after that event she was able to convey to me the sheer horror her father had experienced that day and described the long terms effects on him; for many years afterwards he had constant nightmares. These accounts of war only exist through the personal testimony of relatives: they are rarely found in official records.

The next stop for Private Francis was Norvals Point and from here they moved onto Bloemfontein where they looted a Boer farm. Presumably whatever they took was gone by the next day as he records they had to march twenty-seven miles on merely two biscuits and a pint of coffee and then sleep without blankets or coats. He did stay for two months round Bloemfontein and was fortunate not to have been infected by the enteric outbreak there. However, it was on reaching Pretoria that he at last fell prey to dysentery. Too ill to do duty, he was hospitalised and it was decided to send him home. However, because the railway line had been blown up he was diverted to the Nole Hospital in Johannesburg. Having made a recovery he rejoined his company and in early October he was involved in attacking a Boer laager. He and a comrade became separated and were ambushed. He was hit by four bullets, one in the head, one through the right ear and two in the neck. The Boers took his rifle but they did tie his neck up for him. One comrade was killed and the other taken prisoner but later released. In intense pain Private Francis was taken up to the farm to be cared for and after his wounds were dressed he was given an egg in milk. The major, captain and corporal all praised his bravery. He was eventually brought home on 8 March but not before contracting another serious stomach complaint and having both eyes bitten by mosquitoes. His diary records that many of his fellows died on the return journey, although it does not say whether of wounds or illness.

Sol Plaatje was a highly-educated African who spoke eight languages and kept a diary of his time in Mafeking during the siege. He was central to the action and acted as the official interpreter to the British. It paints a stark picture of how different things were for black people there. A summary form of justice was meted out during the siege. Hence, an African found guilty of stealing would first be flogged but by a third offence would be executed. Plaatje would be the official interpreter for these 'trials'. **Robert Baden-Powell,** later founder of the Scout

The Call for Volunteers and the Besieged Towns

Movement, was in command at Mafeking. He worked out a system of rationing food for the black people. In most cases they had produced the food but he commandeered it and later sold it back at higher prices. Once they reached the stage where horses had to be slaughtered then they found that oat bran and mealies could be mixed with the horse stew to form a soup called 'sowen' which the hungry Africans stood in line for. This was not for all of the black population but only for those Africans considered necessary for the economy. In Thomas Pakenham's book, quoting directly from Baden-Powell's own staff diary, he details on a regular basis how the rations will last for each group, black and white. The calculation was precise and by his reckoning showed that there was only fifteen days food left for black people in contrast to 134 days for the white population. By the beginning of January 1900 he introduced a system of rationing whereby white people could get their food on credit but the natives had to pay up front. As the siege went on, testimony from descendants of the natives in Mafeking recalled being told that their grandparents went to the river and ate mud just to have something in their stomachs! A journalist called W. M. Neill who was in Mafeking wrote for the *Pall Mall Gazette*. 'The sufferers were mostly little boys, mere infants ranging from four or five upwards and hunger had them in its grip and many were black spectres and living skeletons, their ribs literally breaking their shrivelled skin, men, women and children. Probably hundreds died from starvation and associated diseases. Many were found dead on the veldt. Words cannot portray the scene of misery; five or six hundred human frameworks dressed in tattered rags standing in line each holding an old blackened can waiting to crawl patiently to the soup kitchen where the food was distributed.' **Robert Slattery** and his comrades arrived in Mafeking shortly after its relief. With toes out of their shoes and hungry like 'half starved rats', the British soldiers, sent to relieve the town, were suffering too although from lesser privations than the Africans. However, they were clearly in terrible condition and hardly well equipped to fight.

When the Relief of Mafeking on 18 May was finally announced in Britain during theatre performances people stood up, singing the national anthem and cheering. The scenes of wild celebration caused the town's name to enter the English language for a while as synonym for any riotous celebration. Through newspapers people in Britain were almost as well acquainted with the situation in South Africa as we are today through the 24-hour news agenda. The war was at the end of the long reign of Queen Victoria where the British Empire had stretched from end to end of the globe. It was unthinkable that her army could be beaten by a bunch of farmers but previous losses in this war had caused great anxiety. The shadow of Black Week the previous December hung heavily and was lifted little by little as each siege ended. Mafeking became the symbol of that relief and people were euphoric. It is doubtful whether any of those celebrating at home would have read accounts like W. M. Neill's in the *Pall Mall Gazette*. Their eyes were firmly on restoring the pride of the country and the Queen who had ruled over their British Empire for so long. What they knew of the native peoples of the country would have been limited and imbued with a sense of their inferiority as a race.

Once Ladysmith was relieved it was not long before Buller took his men the approximately 150 miles to Bloemfontein with just one major battle to fight on the way. This, the Battle of Driefontein took place on 10 March 1900 and saw fierce fighting all day. The British suffered eighty-two men killed and 342 wounded. One of these was **Albert Peter Morgan**, a 22-year-old resident of Willenhall, Staffordshire. Previously of the South Staffordshire Militia, he had joined the East Kent Volunteers in July 1899. Clearly well-liked locally, he had been accompanied by some forty friends when he took the train for Aldershot. His death was recorded in the local paper in a poem written in tribute by Thomas Bratt whose praise of Mafeking we will see a little later.

The Call for Volunteers and the Besieged Towns

OUR FALLEN TOWNSMAN's FAREWELL
Farewell my tender parents
Dear
Though I have passed away,
Yet in that bright and better land
I hope we'll meet some day.

I fought and died for England's cause
Upon the battlefield
And only unto death itself
Did I my courage yield.
The comrades who fought by my side
They shed their blood for
England's Queen
Most gallantly and true.
Farewell my sisters,
Brothers, too,
And comrades everyone,
If lost this fight on earth, I Hope
A crown of life I've won.

No doubt the thought that he had died for a higher cause would have brought comfort to Private Morgan's family with. But it was written in the first person, although that young man had died and the poet had neither faced the trauma of war nor that of losing a child. The tone differs from the mother's bereavement cited earlier which is taken from the point of view of the grieving mother. In this the words are written on behalf of the dead soldier talking of sadness but emphasising the glory of the death.

On reaching Bloemfontein Buller rested his troops in the town whilst waiting for supplies to be replenished. A force was sent to help in the relief Mafeking on 18 May but it wasn't until 6 June that the army moved to take the Boers' capital of Pretoria. It seems that the Boers decided not to put up a fight here and left their capital with a few families left behind.

The capture of Pretoria seemed to make the British victory complete. At the Relief of Mafeking just two weeks before *The Hampshire Telegraph and Naval Chronicle* had headlined: 'War Practically over as far as the Free State is concerned.' With Pretoria in British hands the *Birmingham Post* on 7 June describes joyous scenes both there and in the capital. In Birmingham people took to the streets around the council house in what sounded like a mixture of a demonstration and a dance. Musical instruments were played loudly and people surged backwards and forwards shouting and whooping with joy. Celebrations in London spread to the suburbs with people hanging Union Jacks from trees and surging into the streets in delight. The patriotism of the times was reflected in the names given to babies after these British victories. Both girls and boys were given the names Kimberley, Ladysmith, Mafeking and Pretoria, usually as middle names but quite frequently as Christian names. This practice was common across the country and certainly popular in working-class areas. In Hackney Catherine Pretoria Beaton, daughter of a cigar maker, was one of six children. Emily Mafeking Aiken, whose father was a pork butcher, lived in Stepney. Jennie Mafeking Anner's father was a railway stoker and they lived in Lewisham.

Poetry too was written to celebrate these victories. Thomas Bratt, dubbed the 'Portobello poet' because of the area of Wolverhampton he came from, was prolific in his writings. Born in the 1850s he began writing poetry in his early thirties. His subjects ranged from the Cup Final where Wolves played Everton in 1893, to a critique of landlords evicting tenants. However, it was during this war that his poetry reached heights of patriotism on the subject of the British righteous cause in South Africa. Below is a poem he wrote whilst Mafeking was still under siege.

The Call for Volunteers and the Besieged Towns

MAFEKING
In a far off distant land
Stands a famous little town.
There a gallant British band,
They have gained themselves renown.
But the Boers around the place,
Still to their entrenchments cling
Often wishing to disgrace
Those defending Mafeking.
But their courage often fails
When attempting such a thing.
Everyman knows what it entails,
Ere he captures Mafeking.
What a noble stand they've made.
Though outnumbered by the foe.
Britons are not yet afraid
Africa's uncrowned king must know.
When they've tired with all their might
Then they've felt the bayonets sting.
Powell and his men can fight
And defend our Mafeking.
Who'll begrudge this hero praise
Or his brave and gallant men
Though shut up one hundred days
In this isolated den.
For these heroes brave and true
Let these heroes brave and true
Let their names not fade with years
Those who've fought for me and you.[10]

Bratt has been called 'the William McGonagall of the Midlands', and it is easy to see why with his grandiose and high-minded language. There is no doubt his poems both reflected and amplified patriotic feelings at this time.

Troops had continued to pour into South Africa throughout the period. Troop ships were leaving continually from a number of ports including Tilbury, Southampton and Plymouth. **R. W. Mourant**, a former pupil at Brighton Grammar School, describes the journey.

> I was in the first ship to leave. We have on board five hundred men and there isn't room to swing a cat. We are divided into messes of eight men, seven sleep in hammocks and the other on a table. Of course we take it in turns to sleep on the table. When we are in our hammocks we touch one another and it isn't at all hot! Two of us are orderlies each week. The duties are to get grub, clean all our mess utensils and straighten up. Of course we scrub tables and forms etc. We drill every morning and every afternoon and as soon as we get past St Vincent we shall go in for target shooting. We are only allowed to smoke on deck and then only with covers over the bowls of our pipes to stop sparks. We must not spit on deck or even over the sides but only in the tubs put there for the purpose. I have a flute here, another of the 19th a tambourine and another a set of bones so when it gets dark we get up concerts. It is fine fun; there is one on now just over my head.

When they arrived at Cape St Vincent they were not allowed ashore as two other troopships were already there and the officers could not trust their men ashore. However, he seemed happy to buy 'grand oranges, fifty for a shilling and bananas six for a penny'. He says 'The islands appear to be of volcanic nature as not a blade of grass could we see on any although they said they had fine orangeries a few miles inland.'

Albert Theaker from Sheffield describes training and drilling in the snow at Chatham barracks. Having passed muster his pay increased from 8d a day to two shillings ha'penny. The voyage to

The Call for Volunteers and the Besieged Towns

South Africa took about twelve days and usually required refuelling and resupplying in such exotic places as the Canary Islands. Mr Theaker records that having left Chatham on 11 February in the snow they reached Las Palmas on 16 March and it was very hot. He recounts that there was a lady there who would sing for the troops and Albert says if you gave her a shilling you could kiss her. Whether there was more than kissing he doesn't say! It was said that the money went to the Absent-Minded Beggar's Fund, a charity to raise money for the troops. Other soldiers sailing for South Africa describe these half-way stops at such places as Tenerife and Cape St Vincent. Tales of the locals hauling up bananas and peaches in baskets to sell to the soldiers capture this exotic atmosphere. Thus these early adventures in a foreign clime were a pleasant prelude to the trip and would no doubt be savoured in the grim days to come.

On arrival in Durban he describes that there were 'lots of niggers [a racist term widely used at that time]' loading boats and later says 'the native police look funny in blue dress, bare feet and a big stick'. Such attitudes are shocking to the modern ear but they would have been accepted by many in a world where Britain had the largest empire in the world and where most of its subjects were people of colour. In the summer of 1899 an exhibition called 'Savage South Africa' had taken place at Earl's Court in London. Men and women had been brought from South Africa to be displayed effectively as a human zoo. No wonder the British soldiers regarded the people they encountered as somehow inferior. When the High Commissioner to the country, Alfred Milner, himself referred to the locals as 'niggers' what better could be expected from the ordinary British private?

By the time Albert Theaker and his comrades reached Pietermaritzburg they found plenty of wounded men and were told by others 'you will want to come back soon'. At Frere, Estcourt and Colenso they witnessed dozens of graves from men killed at Ladysmith. It was an inauspicious start. Their first task was to make a road to transport two naval guns near Lombards Kop and from there to make a road across the ford. They travelled between Boer farms, taking prisoners from them, and then moved on to repairing a railway tunnel which had been blown up by the Boers. Local sabotage was a feature of this warfare and it seemed the British soldiers were constantly trying to repair the damage.

In the midst of this frustration he managed to pal up with a fellow Sheffield man one day who offered him a nip of rum. That 'nip' developed into many nips and he says he didn't know if he was on his head or his feet. By his own description he was a 'hopeless case of drunk'. No doubt his head suffered but it must have been a relief to let go in the middle of the conflict. On 24 June he bumped into an old pal called Bob Ashton and they talked over old times when Bob played the piano at home. No alcohol is mentioned there but the pleasure in their conversation is clear.

There are some small skirmishes with the Boers and work continued on the railway to improve communications. Then on 2 September an officer, who came to inspect their unit, asked him to hold the reins of his horse which shied and dragged Theaker along the ground. He was injured badly enough to be taken to hospital in a cart and he was laid up until 24 September. Just three months earlier he'd agreed with a staff member who'd said their officer was 'off his head' and no doubt this experience would have reinforced his view. It is evident that the gulf between men and officers in this war was vast. The officer class had been to the best public schools and received their commissions often with little military training. This had always been the case but the difference now was that with universal education, the ordinary Tommy had learnt to write and could record his feelings about such matters.[11] We see the same feelings expressed in the writings of **Private Shortland**, another Sheffield man.

Mr Theaker was fortunate in the end to have a only a short

The Call for Volunteers and the Besieged Towns

tour of duty and sailed home in early November having received a handshake and personal thanks from General Buller. Theaker's attitude to the natives was borne out of an Imperial mindset where black people were seen as lesser beings. They acted as scouts in this conflict for both sides since they knew the country well and how to navigate their way at night by the stars but were not really given the respect they deserved. However, we do not have the feeling that he would do anything to directly harm them.

One story I was told by a relative has a significantly darker aspect. **Henry Arthur Burn** from Swansea, a volunteer in the 2nd Battalion of the Welsh Regiment, shot dead a native for stealing copper telegraph wire. This story was recounted to his young grandson when he showed him the pipe that had been made from the stolen wire, remarking that this was very expensive pipe because it lost a man his life. He was also happy to relate how he shot at children for taking pumpkins. It seems clear that Henry Burn was not a well-loved man in the family as his grandson recounted that it was his choice to volunteer when his wife had two children and was heavily pregnant with another. He guarded the railway near Nelspruit and then was involved in drives pushing the Boers towards the blockhouse lines. He returned home on 27 May 1902 just before the end of the war and resumed his work as an engineer at Vivian's of Swansea. I am grateful to his grandson for his candour in telling me this story.

Of course, there are tales too of how Boer farmers treated their black servants. Leslie Mounsfield of Brighton says:

> They make the natives do the work and give them mealie to eat and a nominal pay of 5 shillings or 10 shillings per month or sheep to the value of which payment very rarely comes apparently. I have had talks with heaps of Basutos who have worked for Dutch farmers and their tales all seem to agree as well as I can understand them. One told me that there were three good Dutchmen. It is rather difficult to get

a Basuto to say much as they are so timid. They are prepared to agree with every suggestion one makes but after a time they get confidence and sometimes excited and they talk about sjambok [a leather whip] and shooting and sometimes throat cutting when they talk about the treatment they get.

In August Mourant arrived in Pretoria, over two months after its liberation. He says they had no idea why they were being moved up although he is more than happy when they received bags of back mail and newspapers that had been waiting for them. It is interesting to read his observations of the town. 'Pretoria is certainly a sight for sore eyes after all the towns we have seen. The railway comes winding in, taking here, as throughout the whole journey, the line of least resistance, even at the expense of making long detours; in fact we have not been through a tunnel since leaving Cape Town. The town appears to have some exceedingly nice residences and there are quite a lot (relatively) of trees. It is surrounded on all sides by hills which makes one think the Boers could have held it a long time if they had had sufficient pluck.'

It is this apparent abandonment of their capital which convinced the British that they had secured victory and that the Boers were a spent force. However, this was a misunderstanding of the Boer psyche. They were farming people who thrived on their farms and the open land. They ranged across the veldt on horseback and were expert marksmen, a skill required to keep them safe from wild animals. It was a skill that would enable them to continue fighting for another two years.

Chapter 4

THE WAR AT HOME

The naming of children after victories in the war was only a small part of the patriotism engendered by the conflict. A consequence of the 1870 Education Act was that most people could read and newspapers were popular. News reports stirred patriotic feelings for the soldiers fighting on the veldt. Charitable organisations developed owing to the patriotism engendered by this conflict. At the commencement of operations there was a large outpouring of philanthropic support for both English refugees in the Transvaal and for the soldiers themselves. One of the first to rise to the challenge was the writer and poet Rudyard Kipling. His poem 'The Absent-Minded Beggar' was recited by him and many others on a tour of the country to enthusiastic audiences .Collections were taken at each performance:

> When you've shouted 'Rule Britannia' – when you've sung
> 'God save the Queen'
> When you've finished killing Kruger with your mouth –
> Will you kindly drop a shilling in my little tambourine
> For a gentleman in khaki ordered South?

Throughout the war this poem was recited or sung in all corners of the country. At the Alhambra Music Hall in Leicester Square, London, Arthur Sullivan sang in front of a map of South Africa illustrating the battles that had taken place. A new patriotic song, 'Our Flag', was introduced at this performance. In Wrexham,

North Wales, the *Advertiser* reported that a meeting exhorted donations and stated they wanted 'To look after the women and "kids" of our gallant soldiers and keep them from the workhouse'. It is worth noting that without other support this was the only option for the families who had fought for Queen and country. It was reported that a lady in a shop refused to take her change and suggested that the shop set up a collection for the soldiers. This idea caught on and soon collections were started in many shops nearby. There are many other examples which include the following:

- In the Diocese of Watling in Oxfordshire collections were raised in twenty-six churches. When Ladysmith was first besieged by the Boers, people rushed to buy the newspapers to keep up with the drama. A working men's club in Oxford raised another collection.
- In Liverpool the Smoking Club gave a recitation of 'The Absent-Minded Beggar' and raised £2 and 5 shillings.
- In Padstow, Cornwall £3 was raised for The Soldiers, Sailors and Armed Forces Association (the SSAFA) and a dance followed the collection with, once again, a recitation of Kipling's poem. The Gowongo Minstrels arrived in Padstow on 27 December 1899 and £3 and 3 shillings was raised, some of which was paid to the County Fund, the treasurer of which was Miss Gertrude Prideaux-Brune, a member of the local aristocracy. The popularity of men blacking-up and singing minstrel songs was on the increase at this time but in view of the context of a war being fought in Africa it is interesting to note that it was used as a fundraiser.
- In Scotland the *Aberdeen Weekly Journal* reported on a fund established 'for those who were left behind'. Presenting a long list of contributors in the newspaper, it had already collected £1,900 by mid-November 1899 or 1900.
- Again at the Alhambra Music Hall in London, a ballet on the

theme had been devised depicting the day in the life of a Tommy beginning at sunrise and ending at sunset. It was aptly named 'Soldiers of the Queen'.
- The *Liverpool Mercury* reported an illustrated lecture with patriotic music, photos of South African heroes and a cinematographic representation of the departure of the troops.
- A novel approach was undertaken in Middlesbrough whereby a graphologist, Madame Dore, offered to analyse people's handwriting for sixpence. This appeal to vanity proved very popular and in a short space of time in March 1900 had raised just over £479.
- Meanwhile in the Isle of Wight people tried to mimic the war itself with a reenactment called 'Assault at Arms'.

Everywhere in Britain people were doing something to support the war effort. On 27 November 1899 the *Bristol Mercury* reported a concert in St Agnes Church, St Paul's, Bristol which was concluded with an oration given by the Reverend T. Harvey. He spoke warmly of the sacrifice of the widows and exhorted his listeners to take responsibility for them. There is no doubt that there was an abundance of goodwill.

Enthusiasm for supporting the war effort was enormous. Within ten days of the launch of the Lord Mayor of London's fund some £135,000 had been contributed for refugees fleeing the Transvaal, many of whom would have been the gold-prospecting 'Uitlanders'. A plethora of charities sprang up at this time but co-ordination between them was poor or even non-existent. Within a month the editor of *Truth*, a periodical founded by Henry Labouchère in 1877, complained: 'It strikes me and will probably strike everyone who studies the facts that we are suffering from a plethora of relief funds. I do not mean there is too much cash or too many collectors but there are too many distributing agencies at work.' Well-meaning charities and individuals struggled with the task of relieving soldiers and their families in a major war. This was exacerbated by the fact that this war was being fought 6,000 miles away

By the end of the war the Lord Mayor's Fund had raised over £1 million, of which the Red Cross received £99,000, the Royal Patriotic Fund £493,000 and the SSAFA approximately £500,000. It is worth explaining the role of the Patriotic Fund which had been established at Queen Victoria's instigation at the time of the Crimean War in 1855. It was a charitable fund set up by Royal Warrant to support widows and orphans from that conflict. Constituted in that way, it had a unique role and its president was Prince George, the Duke of Cambridge. Given that role it is interesting to note a report in the *Daily News* from 17 February 1900 which reports that in 1897 the fund was well provisioned. However, it was decided to make grants to widows of old soldiers of the Crimea who had returned home safe and had 'died in their beds thus depleting the fund'. It was two years before the outbreak of hostilities but by then tension was high following the Jameson Raid of 1895 and it is curious that no foresight was exercised concerning the possibility of war. It appears a universal truth that lack of preparation for armed conflict and support for the relatives of soldiers and their families is a feature of warfare.

The Lord Mayor's Fund was originally launched for refugees in South Africa but at the urging of the Duke of Cambridge it was extended to include wounded and disabled soldiers and their families. He announced: 'I therefore propose, in order to give the public the widest scope for their benevolence, that contributions for widows, orphans and other dependents of these who lose their lives, shall be handed to the Patriotic Fund Commission; those for the sick and wounded to the British Red Cross Society; those for soldiers disabled by their wounds (for their benefit after they leave the service) to that excellent organisation Lloyds Patriotic Fund and for those wives and children separated to SSAFA.'

The War at Home

For the very first time we see national newspapers setting up charitable funds. The *Daily Mail* and the *Daily Telegraph* both encouraged contributions from their readers. They published a running record of the men who died, their regiments and how many children they had. These dependants were helped through annuities and interestingly the fund did not automatically discriminate against widows who remarried, noting that their husbands had made the final sacrifice for their country and their wives had suffered as a result. The Transvaal Widows Fund took a different approach.

Despite all these generous efforts there were intrinsic problems with the funding arrangements. The agencies found it difficult to work together. At a local level there was the feeling that 'our troops should be helped in their own towns and villages'. At a national level problems arose as different agencies operated with different perspectives. The Charity Organisation Society (founded by Helen Bosanquet and Octavia Hill in 1869) was unhappy that wives and widows had to depend on charities and argued that soldiers' pay should be increased to make provision for dependents: 'It is far from creditable to a great Empire that immediately our forces are called into action, the wives and children should become applicants for relief from the charitably disposed; and if the service is to be really popular the community at large must in the form of increased allowances to the individual soldier take this burden upon itself.' The lack of coordination and co-operation was commented on early in the war in *Truth*: 'The whole position of the War Relief Funds and agencies is a discreditable muddle and no better service could be rendered to our soldiers and sailors at the present juncture than by taking steps at once to organise one general and comprehensive scheme which would put the business of collecting money and administering relief on an intelligent and business like footing.'

A few months later the Select Committee on War Funds called

for central and local committees to be established to co-ordinate activities centrally and in different towns. In February 1900 a conference was called under the presidency of the Prince of Wales but nothing came of it.[1] Then towards the end of 1900 the Royal Patriotic Fund tentatively suggested that a Central Patriotic Fund be set up to coordinate the work of the various bodies engaged in charitable war work but again this proposal did not progress. It was noted by an official at the war office that 'for one reason or another the bodies are at variance and in two or three cases, at least, distinctively hostile to the Patriotic Fund'.

In Chapter 3 Captain Mary Murray of the Salvation Army recounted her experiences in the early part of the war. Whilst her prime motivation was in promoting a Christian message she worked practically among the troops and saw some of the grimmest sights in the trenches. She recognised early on that young men were being afflicted with rheumatism from sleeping on hard, wet ground.

As has been shown, one organisation that became active at this time was the SSAFA. Originally founded in 1885 by Colonel Sir James Gildea to look after hard-pressed families when soldiers were serving abroad, it was now to look after the veterans themselves especially those injured in war. Prince Christian, grandson-in-law of Queen Victoria, was an enthusiastic supporter of this cause and his wife Princess Christian became patron in 1899. The organisation undertook a 'casework' approach and its aim was to 'befriend the soldier or sailor on sick furlough or on discharge in every possible way'. Its objectives were:

- To help serving and ex-servicemen (and women) by providing them with the name and address of a 'friend' in each parish ward throughout the Empire to whom they may be commended on discharge for aid in employment or other forms of help suited to their needs.
- To establish and maintain permanent convalescent homes to

The War at Home

contribute to the support of disabled ex-servicemen (and women) in their homes if considered necessary.
- To teach useful trades and train in skills men who have been discharged from the Services as medically unfit.
- In time of war to arrange accommodation for as many sick and wounded convalescent servicemen (and women) in temporary convalescent homes and private houses as possible.

Setting up a nationwide network of friends facilitated an effective casework approach. Within a short space of time some 16,000 volunteers had been recruited and enabled to give advice, cash, clothes or assistance in finding employment. As Julian Paget says in his book *No Problem Too Difficult : A History of the Forces Help Society*: 'There was no welfare state then, no Department of Social Security and no national pension scheme with the result that many old soldiers faced very real hardship . . .'[2] The Chairman of the SSAFA said in 1902: 'Many must go, at least temporarily to the wall; their suffering will be part of the price of war, not the least part of it.' Between 1903 and 1908 120,602 were found by the Society as being in need of help and £49,000 was distributed in grants.

The Society (as the SSAFA was referred to), very much encouraged by Prince and Princess Christian, introduced the idea of Homes of Rest for Disabled Soldiers. The first were started in Bisley, Surrey in 1899 on land donated by Lord Pirbright, where four homes, each housing sixteen men, were established. Others followed and the Society took over an existing home in Portsmouth whose aim was to maintain and care for sailors or soldiers who were disabled through age or infirmity.

The role of organising convalescent homes for the wounded was undertaken with great determination. While the war continued some 200 homes were established and over 2,000 men were sent to recover from their wounds. Others convalescing at home were paid six shillings or ten shillings a week if they were married. The average weekly wage was, at that time, approximately nineteen shillings a week.

By contrast there is an intriguing plaque in York Minster which was dedicated to the 18th Hussars (Queen Mary's Own). It reads: 'On the return of the regiment from the war comrades and friends dedicated two cottage homes to the memories of those who fell. Since they failed to fulfil their object they were sold and this memorial substituted, the balance of the proceeds being devoted to the assistance of old soldiers of the regiments in trouble or distress. October 1914.' It seems surprising, given the number of casualties named on the memorial opposite the minster, that these cottage homes were not occupied by those in need. Since cottage homes attached to other organisations were used it begs the question as to what was offered to veterans in those in York.

It shouldn't be presumed that the whole country was fully in support of the war. In fact, two major groupings formed in opposition to the war. One was led by Leonard Courtney, a Liberal MP, who opposed the war and favoured negotiation to bring it to a close. The other was led by the campaigning journalist W.T. Stead, who argued that the war should be brought to an end immediately. Keir Hardie, of the nascent Independent Labour Party, was also in opposition to the conflict and he visited South Africa in this period. They were all dubbed pro-Boers by newspapers such as the *Daily Mail*. Meetings were organised around the country and, in a world aroused by war fever, these were often disrupted. An interesting example of this occurred in Liskeard in July 1900. It is worth noting that one of the speakers at this meeting was Emily Hobhouse. Her uncle was Leonard Courtney MP and it was Emily who later went to South Africa to see the conditions in the concentration camps for herself. Alongside her was a Miss Ellen Robinson from Liverpool as well as the Liberal MP for Carnarvon, Lloyd George. The meeting was

The War at Home

presided over by the well-known author, Mr A. T. Quiller-Couch. Despite this illustrious platform the meeting did not proceed well. Before the meeting 'Imperialist' literature had been circulated in the town and a lively crowd had gathered. While waiting for the meeting to start the crowd sang patriotic airs and loudly cheered Private Webber of the 2nd Devon and Cornwall Light Infantry who had travelled from the village of Hessenford and attended the meeting in uniform.

Emily Hobhouse tried to speak above the tumult and compared this meeting with others she had addressed in Leicester, Leeds, Bradford, Liverpool and Manchester. She was horrified to return home to her native Cornwall and find this disruption. It was only when she spoke of the bravery of people at the relief of Mafeking that she was given a respectful hearing. But this changed when she said that those using the National Anthem to bring down a meeting could not follow the brave example set by those at the Siege of Mafeking. Lloyd George was not afforded a hearing at all and uproar ensued when a party of young men, many bearing miniature Union Jacks, stormed the platform and the meeting was broken up.[3]

As the war intensified and news of the 'scorched earth' and concentration camp policies had reached home, Lloyd George took his opposition to Birmingham. On 18 December 1901 a meeting was organised there, which was the home territory of Joseph Chamberlain, the Colonial Secretary and one of the main architects of policy on South Africa. Lloyd George's family had already suffered for his views, his wife being snubbed by friends and his son had to leave his preparatory school because of bullying. That day at Birmingham Town Hall, he was met with an angry mob yelling 'Traitor', 'Pro Boer'. Not allowed to speak at all, he had to be rescued by the police who dressed him in a policeman's uniform, a disguise considered necessary for his own safety. A photo of this occasion is exhibited at Birmingham Town Hall as a notable incident in local history.

Chapter 5

THE SICKNESS TOOK THEM

A shocking fact is that more men died of disease in the Boer War than on the battlefield. Enteric, caused by polluted water, was the main killer but pneumonia, diphtheria, meningitis and eryisipelas (a bacterial skin infection) added to the toll. Death also arose from sunstroke, accidental discharge of firearms and one poor fellow was taken by a crocodile!

In August 1900, at the height of the South African winter, **R. W. Mourant** of the City Imperial Volunteers was writing home from the vicinity of Pretoria and said: 'Two nights we had were the worst I've had out here. No food, heavy thunderstorms and severe frosts. In one night over three hundred trek oxen pegged out from wet and cold. We also lost one officer and several men killed by cold and two drowned in Bronkhurst Spruit.' Mourant was another one of the ex-Brighton Grammar School boys whose letters home illuminate graphically what life was like for the soldiers. Reading of men freezing to death must have been a shock for the families back home.

In December 1900 a young private from the Lancashire Fusiliers was found at daybreak lying dead in a pool of water, still holding his rifle. Dennis Devine, an ex-miner, was just twenty years old. His commanding officer wrote: 'People should know these are the conditions we suffer.'[1] However, it was the enteric that ravaged the army: even the medics who were sent to tend to them were not spared. During the day South Africa is a hot country and troops needed water in copious supplies. On the

The Sickness Took Them

move and in camp it was not readily accessible except from streams and rivers. The streams were often muddy similar to those at home but in this war-torn country there was another hazard; that of dead bodies contaminating the water. These could be Boer, British or native. An officer recorded: 'Native cemeteries are apt to become a danger to public health. At Modder River a large number of graves from a neighbouring refugee camp was found to be situated on the edge of the river where an intake of water supply is taken for the troops.' The water of the Modder River was polluted too by the dead bodies of horses and soldiers from the battle at Paardeberg at the end of February. This was upriver from Bloemfontein where Buller's troops came to rest just fourteen days later. All of this was compounded by a victory by the Boers at Sannas Post who then took control of Bloemfontein's water supply. Later still there were to be dead livestock from Boer farms which had been destroyed by the British as part of the 'Scorched Earth' policy. The same officer continues: 'Carcasses left on the veldt have been disembowelled and left to dry in the sun.' The spread of disease would have been rampant by this time.

Private Ince from Hindley in Lancashire wrote home to his father: 'We had no water in our water bottles. When we stopped there was a pit with water in. Well we called it water but you would not if you had seen it. It was so white it looked like soapsuds and there was a dead horse in it too. It tasted good all the same.'[2] An enteric outbreak took hold with a vengeance after Buller's troops took Bloemfontein on 13 March 1900. After the exhausting fight for Ladysmith the troops were given some respite in the town whilst the army reprovisioned but with a dubious water source the disease flourished. This illness had affected the troops almost since the beginning of the war. As mentioned previously, Mr Heward, the railway worker in Ladysmith had talked of men becoming sick after drinking from the streams in the local hills.

The Royal Navy had played a major part in this conflict, bringing in heavy guns by sea and hauling them to the battlefield. **Henry Gardner** was a nineteen-year-old stoker who had been a labourer in Bermondsey, a poor area of South London. The Reverend Andrew Mearns, cited in Chapter 1, had written of the poverty in Bermondsey. His photo shows him to be a young man of slight build. Arriving in Durban in October 1899 he saw little action before he was taken ill with enteric and had to be moved from the tented sick bay to the hospital at Intombi. He had fought the sickness for between two and three months and had just began to recover when an abscess that had developed on his throat killed him. The conditions were so poor they were considered a scandal; Winston Churchill, who'd reported from Spion Kop, highlighted the fact that food and comforts intended for the sick soldiers were diverted to some of the officers in Ladysmith.

Private J. E. Shortland from Sheffield arrived in Durban with the York and Lancashire regiment on 24 January 1900, the day of the Battle of Spion Kop. He was taken ill with enteric almost immediately and was out of action for fourteen days. Having recovered, he was involved in the relief of Ladysmith. A telegram arrived from the Queen congratulating them all on the relief of the town and he contrasts this with the attitude of the officers to the ordinary soldiers. He is angry when he recounts that 'the soldiers were made to get up without drink and march with no water in their waterbottles' while they had watched their officer have as good a breakfast as he had at home. There is no doubt that the officer class expected privileged treatment and deference to their status. Private Shortland comments bitterly that the officers treat 'Tommy Atkins' like schoolchildren, echoing the words of Mr Heward, the railway worker from Ladysmith and his fellow Yorkshireman, Theaker from Sheffield who featured in the previous chapter.[3]

Many officers had servants in the field. One such was Lieutenant Navarine Fellowes from South Hams in Devon. Having attended

The Sickness Took Them

the United Service College in Bideford, Devon he began a military career. Whilst serving with the West India Regiment on 17 November 1901 he died in a battle or skirmish with the Boers and his manservant Tierney died by his side. His fellow officers erected a memorial which said he'd bravely carried on shooting to the end. The military records on the Ancestry.co.uk website state that Private Tierney was 'killed accidentally'. There is no interpretation of what happened. It certainly appears that the manservant of an officer was expected to be by his side without question.

Later, during the army's sojourn at Bloemfontein, enteric set in with a vengeance. Private Charles Ireland, originally from Devonport, was brought up in an orphanage in nearby Brixham. He was serving with the First West Riding Regiment and describes the outbreak in Bloemfontein: 'At this place we shortly knew the dangers soldiers have to put up with on service. Our men were carried by threes and fours to be attended by doctors for dysentery. Every afternoon we could see fourteen or fifteen funerals at the cemetery gates.'[4]

Captain Mary Murray of the Salvation Army visited Bloemfontein at the height of the epidemic there in 1900. She heard from a lieutenant that 150 soldiers had been buried there in May alone and was distressed to see the makeshift nature of those burials. There were no coffins; each lad was wrapped in a blanket and they were laid side by side in a communal grave. This cemetery, which had been for the inhabitants of Bloemfontein, where funerals were part of the rhythm of life but usually reserved for the elderly and very young, was now being taken over by the burials of young British soldiers. She remarked that the 'Kaffir' workmen were kept busy not just with picks and shovels but crowbars to break up the earth for more graves, such was the condition of the ground!

An interesting insight into how the hospitals sought to cope with this never-ending tide of illness is provided in the diary of a nursing orderly at the hospital in Bloemfontein. He describes how the smell in the ward is very foul having been closed all night. Then he goes on to tell us that breakfast is not until 10.00 a.m. as the milk has first to be 'scalded'. This was presumably unpasteurised milk. Recovering patients who have had a normal temperature for ten to twelve days are allowed a first meal of minced chicken in milk. Then at three in the afternoon patients have arrowroot or lemonade followed by custard and then barley water. The patients are also allowed to smoke. To modern eyes this might sound the opposite of convalescence but in the middle of a worrying epidemic in a war zone the soldiers would see this as their welcome relaxation.[5]

The medics who came to tend to the sick and wounded could also fall prey to the terrible illness themselves. A hospital set up to help in South Africa was raised in Wales. Funded by private and voluntary funds, it equipped a hospital ship that set sail on 14 April 1900. There was Major Cockerill of the RAMC, Professor Jones from Victoria University, Manchester, three senior surgeons, two assistant surgeons, eight medical students and dressers, ten nursing sisters, two maids and forty-eight orderlies. Alfred rose to become professor of anatomy at King's College London, but in 1899 journeyed to South Africa to supervise the 'Welsh Hospital'. There, aged thirty-nine, he died, like many others not of wounds but of fever.

Stopping temporarily in Bloemfontein at the height of the enteric outbreak one medical student contracted the illness and died. Moving onto Springfontein where the hospital was to be based they found a 'melancholy place' where obtaining supplies was hindered by the fact that the military had commandeered most of the transport. Nevertheless, the field hospital was established on a westward-facing slope and the staff began operational work. It was a thankless task tending to all the lads suffering from enteric and by just six months later they had packed up and Springfontein was changed to a convalescent hospital. In that short time they had lost three surgeons, one

The Sickness Took Them

doctor and one nurse. Row upon row of British Army graves fill the cemetery at Springfontein, each plain tombstone commemorating the story of a young soldier whose life spanned no more than twenty-one years.[6]

Private Frank Bleach from Cuckfield, Sussex, had joined the Active Service Volunteer Company of his county regiment and died at Bloemfontein on 14 March 1901 of enteric, the day before his thirtieth birthday. A creative young man, he had just started producing a newspaper for his comrades in Bloemfontein. In February 1901 he sent home No 1 of the *Soft Nose*, a weekly paper published by the Sussex Regiment.

Arthur Wilson, referred to in an earlier chapter being at Kimberley and Paardeberg, also witnessed people dying of enteric: 'We were camped at Springfield a short distance out of town. Here our losses of the whole army were terrific from dysentery and enteric fever.' They were rushed from there to deal with the remnants of the disaster at Korn Spruit or Sanna's Post which enabled the Boers to take control of the Bloemfontein's water supply. This loss greatly aggravated the epidemic which led to the deaths of 2,000 soldiers in all.

Noel Seagar, mentioned previously and who describes treating men wounded from Magersfontein, was still working at Wynberg Hospital in April 1900. He wrote home to say:

> We are in the wards hard at it one hundred and eight hours out of one hundred and sixty eight per week. The sickness out here is awful. We have eight hundred beds in this hospital always full up; in fact we can't make room for them fast enough, and all the other general hospitals and hospital ships are the same, although we send two or three shiploads home every week. There are about half a dozen deaths from enteric fever every day and a third of our own men are down with it which makes duty very hard for the remainder.

A fellow Brighton Grammar School pupil, Joe Parsons of Robert's Horse, who wrote an article for the school magazine *Past and Present*, died of dysentery at Wynberg on 25 March. The editor wrote: 'As a pupil at the school he won our esteem and affection, and while his untimely death in the service of our country will be deeply regretted, his memory will long be cherished by all who knew him.' There was no honour in any of these deaths, just the pains of retching and diarrhoea until the body became too dehydrated to carry on.

Water was an issue throughout the campaign and in hot temperatures men were often expected to march without water. **Charles Dunn** from Devon joined the Coldstream Guards aged eighteen in London. By August 1900 he had already been promoted to corporal but was stripped of that rank for helping a private collect water on a twenty-mile march. In a letter to his mother he writes: 'I am a private again. I got reduced for not reporting a man who went to get some water on the march it was very hot and I was thirsty enough to go and get some myself so the officer reported me for not reporting him so I got striped and I did not trouble about it as it is hard for a Corporal out here.'

Dunn was the son of schoolteachers from the village of Halwell in Devon. When he joined up in 1898 aged eighteen his occupation was given as labourer. He saw service in Gibraltar before being drafted to South Africa in May 1900. He was to live the last months of his young life there. We know he had loving parents and a girlfriend called Lizzie who he had met in London whilst serving with the Coldstream Guards. Lizzie sent him a cake, a pair of socks, tobacco, a packet of cocoa, a jar of Bovril, a piece of wedding cake and some sweets. He says: 'So I had a good blow out last night.' You can hear his pleasure thousands of miles from home thinking of his pretty girlfriend and her kindness in packing the parcel. Charles's letters home to his mother enquire about friends and commiserate about the death of an elderly aunt. In August he is already fretting about coming home and by

The Sickness Took Them

October he is expecting that they will return with Lord Roberts who is due to leave Cape Town in a couple of days.

He describes the march to take Komatie Poort in the north-east of the country: 'It was a rough march from Waterfall it was all hills and rivers and ditches we marched the last two days forty miles and last fifteen miles without a drop of water. We had seven die in the Brigade of Guards I was nearly done myself and we only had three quarter of a pound of flour for all the march each day and three quarters lb of meat and no blankets to sleep in we could not get the blankets over the hills'.

He was glad though that they had been moved to Pretoria since enteric had taken hold at Komatie Port and he 'did not want the fever'. He finishes this letter to his mother by saying: 'I don't think I have any more to say at present I will tell you all about it when I come home.' But Charles wasn't to see his family, friends or girlfriend again. The fever he had feared took hold of him and he died on 6 November 1900 of enteric at Standerton Stationary Hospital. Accounts at the National Army Museum tell of the large numbers of young men suffering and dying at Standerton. Many of those at this hospital were Australians who, together with the Canadians and New Zealanders, were fighting alongside the British army.

Ernest Samuel Vigers of the Hussars was at Lydenburg in the north of the country, not so far from Charles Dunn. In late September he wrote to his brother at home: 'I have been offered a job as master tailor in the Pretoria Constabulary and the colonel of the 19th Hussars wants me to transfer to them. But I am not having any. I have seen quite enough of it already. Roll on England. I must now close – you must excuse my bad writing. I have to use my knee for a writing desk.' He had managed to evade the dreaded enteric but he, too, was keen to get home as soon as possible.

There are many memorials to the men who fought and died in the war. They are not as ubiquitous as the stone cross memorials established for the First and Second World Wars but the sites of many can be found by searching online. There are memorials extending from Scotland right down to the far west of Cornwall with all the counties in between. Some are stone monuments in public places, others can be found on plaques inside churches and civic buildings and others within grammar and public schools. There is a variety in the form of these monuments and what they record. Occasionally they list all men from the area who went to war. More usually they commemorate those who died. Given the overwhelming number of men who died from enteric, this is not often recorded, hence the memorial in Sherborne Abbey in Dorset is particularly striking. In this serene and beautiful building the brass plaque which glistens in the sun records ninety non-commissioned officers who died in South Africa. Of these only twenty-four died in action or of wounds; the remaining sixty-six all died of enteric.

Chapter 6

AND THE BOYS WENT TOO

The ranks of the army were swelled by boys, some as young as thirteen. Some, as with their older comrades, joined up because the Queen's shilling was a good incentive to keep them out of rural or urban poverty. Some, however, came from institutions which provided a guaranteed supply of young men for whom entry into the military was predestined. Some children went to orphanages as babies; others later when one or both parents died. It was not uncommon for a widowed parent to place children in an orphanage simply because he or she could not afford to keep them. Industrial schools were another source of recruits. These schools were for wayward boys, mainly just 'street kids'.

Arthur Wilson, who has already been referred to at Kimberley in Chapter 3 wrote an account of his life for his son. He tells of his family headed by his widowed mother:

> We were a large family, ten but only seven grew up, three boys and four girls. We were a happy lot when we were at home together. But our dear mother, being left poorly off, had a struggle to bring us all up and as soon as possible we all started out to earn our own living. My twin brother and I were able to get into the Duke of York's Military school with the ambition of getting into the army as soon as possible which we did at the age of fifteen. Being so young we had to join the Bands of these regiments and being trained as musicians we did not find it come so hard. The life in the band as a boy was hard but happy. In those days

you didn't get a great deal to eat; you supplemented the ration by purchasing things from the Regimental Canteen whenever you had anything to spend and as your pay as a boy was only 6d per day out of which you had to pay Mess 3d per day and also pay for some of your kit as it got worn or lost you weren't able to buy much and often went to bed hungry. But from time to time my dear mother used to send occasional parcels and a little money when the dear soul had it to spare.

He describes learning to ride by being lifted onto the horse as he was so small and having to stand on an inverted bucket to brush the horse's head. Trumpet and bugle practice was compulsory every day. 'A trumpeter in the cavalry has to learn both of these instruments, the trumpet calls being used in barracks and camp, the bugle for calls in the field.'

The photo of the Drummer Boy at Colesberg illustrates graphically the age and immaturity of some recruits. Arthur Wilson tells us of some of the hardships of being a young recruit but when he had leave he had his mother to return to. After a year, by then posted to Newbridge in Ireland, he 'had his first furlough (a month) and naturally went home to London, my dear mother helping me largely with the huge railway and boat fare. I was very proud of myself in my little short jacket and pill box cap perched on the side of my head. I was very ill on the boat each way from Dublin to Holyhead.' It is interesting to see how much the young soldier had to pay to supplement his diet and to return from his posting. Nevertheless, Arthur had a mother to return to on leave. If you were a boy from one of the Industrial Schools or orphans that option was not available to you. These boys, whose fate was decided by the institution they were brought up in, provided ideal cannon fodder for the army.

A plaque at Lewisham Industrial School, now lost in the London blitz, showed that thirty-five of their boys took part in the war and six of them died out there. The Macclesfield Industrial School provided three young men who lost their lives. An eulogy was inscribed on the memorial at Dr Guthrie's Industrial School in Edinburgh: 'Sacred to the memory of men and boys educated in Dr Guthrie's industrial schools who fell in India, Egypt, the Soudan and South Africa fighting for their Queen, King, King and country. They fell with their backs to the veldt and their feet to the foe. Leaving in battle no blot on their name; looking proudly to heaven from their deathbed of fame.'

At the 'Home for Catholic Friendless Youths' in Liverpool it was said: 'Many boys are fighting for us in South Africa, some of them in Ladysmith. Is there not some reward to a nation that takes care of its destitute boys? Can you not see that reward now? Look at South Africa, think of Ladysmith. Many of the lads that you have helped in their adversity are now fighting for Queen and country.'[1]

In an era when population growth was high and so was mortality, many orphanages undertook the raising of children. They were imbued with discipline and received a basic education. For these institutionalised children the army provided an ideal occupation in which they had little say. Grandiose notions of patriotism to justify the life and deaths of these lads was a reflection of the prevailing wisdom.

The Foundling Hospital in central London had been founded in 1739 by Thomas Coram, a returning sea captain, to save destitute babies and children from the streets. Extreme poverty would lead mothers to the desperate measure of abandoning their babies. It was to help with this problem that the Foundling Hospital was endowed. The need was so great that the hospital often could not take all the babies presented. But for those taken in the mother would leave a token, maybe a distinctive piece of material or a piece of cheap jewellery. These were kept so later a link could be made between the mother and child. Once admitted, though, the child would be given a new name.

Up until the age of five the children were sent to wet nurses in the country but after that they were brought back to live at the hospital. Going to school within the institution, segregated by gender and forbidden to speak to each other at mealtimes, the children led a regimented life. The girls were mainly trained to go into domestic service and the boys into the military. Recruiting parties were held whereby commanding officers visited and picked out boys for their regiments, favouring physique and strength. The boys themselves had no say.

Not surprisingly many of those boys went to fight in South Africa. During the period of the Boer War 108 enlisted in the army and of those fifty made that hazardous journey to South Africa. They went with a variety of regiments including the North Staffordshires, the 2nd Battalion Shropshire Light Infantry, the 6th Dragoons and the 18th Hussars. The range of these regiments shows the interest shown by the military in boys from the Foundling Hospital. It is known that at least four died out there. **William Kaye** died serving with the Welsh Regiment at Middleburg on 25 May 1901. **Henry Smart** died in Wynberg Hospital on 11 August 1901. **Samuel Wignell** of the East Kent Regiment and **William Doyle** of the Royal Field Artillery died within a week of each other in Bloemfontein of the dreaded enteric. All four of these boys were resident at the Foundling Hospital when the 1891 census was undertaken. At the time of the census Henry was only eight years old, Herbert was nine and Samuel and William just twelve years old.[2] Who could have foretold that within ten years all would be dead in a country far away fighting for their country which coveted South African gold.

As the Foundlings had no family, upon their deaths their effects, were returned to the Hospital. Hospital records show that the Secretary of State for War presented £21, 2 shillings and 8 pence being the effects of Samuel Wignell and for William Doyle there was the sum of £19, 11 shillings and 5 pence. Both these young men had grown up together and as likely died together in the same hospital in Bloemfontein. William and Samuel were both just twenty-one years old.³

All boys from the Foundling Hospital were customarily followed up in their early employment and depending on recommendations from their masters they received a Good Conduct Payment. In most cases this would be with commanding officers of their regiments. In this period immediately following the Boer War most boys were still with their regiments, some in South Africa and some returned to other postings.

Some of the payments were as follows:

- William Keates who'd been in the Durham Light Infantry in South Africa received 20/- £1.
- Edward Tatham of the 2nd Battalion Shropshire Light Infantry received 17/6d in October 1903.
- Charles Yeatman of the 2nd Battalion Shropshire Light Infantry received 15/- in October 1903.
- Robert Jardine of the 6th (Inniskilling) Dragoons in South Africa received 10/- in September 1903.

George Sparkes of the 3rd Dragoon Guards was not to be rewarded, however, as his Lieutenant Colonel stated that he 'was very dull and sullen tempered'.

Finding later records of the Foundling boys who fought in South Africa is not easy. It is worth remembering that virtually all soldiers who fought are absent from the 1901 census. By the 1911 census spellings may have slightly changed and people were living in unexpected locations. However, of the young men from the 1891 cohort at the hospital who went to fight in South Africa, the following were traceable.

- **Phillip Tilson** of the 1st Durham Light Infantry in South Africa was a Corporal in the same regiment and then serving in India. He was thirty and single.

- **Joseph Kendrick** of the 6th Dragoon Guards in South Africa was serving in the police in Sheffield. He was married with four daughters, two of whom had been born whilst on service in India.
- **Robert Powis** of the 18th Hussars was in the police in West Yorkshire. He was married but sadly their only child had died.

It is interesting that the choice of careers for these 'old boys' was in the services, which would fit well with an institutionalised background.

Albert Skedgell. At 17, he was the youngest sailor to be landed with the Naval Brigades in South Africa. *(Courtesy of Roy Tucker)*

George Ravenhill was awarded the VC at the Battle of Colenso. It was taken from him after he was convicted of a petty theft whilst he and his family were in the workhouse. *(Courtesy of Graham Knight)*

The HMS *Doris* Memorial in Devonport Park, Plymouth. *(Courtesy of Tony Marchese)*

A street in Nechells, Birmingham, the area where George and his family lived in the early 1900s. *(Courtesy of Graham Knight)*

Fred Griffin from Honiton, Devon wrote a journal for his mother whilst living through the Siege of Kimberly. *(Courtesy of Jenny Ridd)*

Robert Slattery from Lancashire helped lift the Siege of Kimberly. *(Courtesy of David Whitehead)*

Henry Gardner from Bermondsey, a stoker in the Royal Navy, died at Intombi Hospital near Ladysmith. As a journalist Winston Churchill wrote about the terrible conditions there. *(Courtesy of John Shalice)*

First page of the letter to Henry's mother informing her of his death. *(Courtesy of John Shalice)*

Charles Dunn, a young soldier in the Coldstream Guards who died of enteric at Standerton Hospital. *(Courtesy of David Yabsley)*

Lizzie Bowcombe, Charles's girlfriend, sent him a parcel of goodies to enjoy. *(Courtesy of David Yabsley)*

British soldiers entering Pretoria in June 1900. It was believed this would bring an end to the conflict but the guerrilla war continued for another two years. *(Courtesy of Western Cape Archives and Library, Cape Town)*

Boy soldier after the Battle of Colesberg. Many very young soldiers participated in this conflict. *(Courtesy of the National Media Museum, Science and Society Picture Library)*

Robert Milburn, the author's great-uncle, as a young recruit to the Coldstream Guards. *(Courtesy of Mary Ann Parkinson)*

Robert pictured with soldiers from the Queen Victoria's Black Watch Guard in South Africa. *(Courtesy of Mary Ann Parkinson)*

Boer women guarding their belongings which they have rescued from their farmhouse. *(Courtesy of Sheila Ashford)*

'Destroyed Boer Farmhouse'. *(Courtesy of Professor Sir Roderick Floud, from Liddell Hart Centre for Military Archives)*

William Duncan, aged five, at school in Dundee. He is third from the right in the front row. *(Courtesy of Malcolm Duncan)*

His father, William Neilson Duncan, had been working in South Africa and joined Kitchener's Fighting Horse in the war. He lost touch eventually and never returned to Scotland. He is third from the right in the second row from the front. *(Courtesy of Malcolm Duncan)*

A ring made from South African gold brought back by John Ball for his sweetheart Bessie. *(Courtesy of Nicola Wills)*

Medals awarded to Tom Randell of the Royal Artillery. Many of the men whose stories are told here won medals. Tom's are for his service in India and the other two are for South Africa. The bars on the ribbon denote awards for individual battles. *(Courtesy of Robert Wall)*

John Ball's son Steve and wife: the family still treasures the ring. *(Courtesy of Nicola Wills)*

Chapter 7

THE BITTER END

When Pretoria was taken on 6 June 1901 the rejoicing at home was immense. The presumption was, of course, that the war was over and that British and Imperial victory was complete. Celebrations took place all over Britain, not least in working-class areas of Scotland and Lancashire from where the army had drawn so many recruits.

This euphoria for the troops was short-lived, however. It is a truism to say that you cannot beat an army on its own territory and the northern provinces of the Orange Free State and the Transvaal were the Boers' own territory. In such an untamed African landscape, wild animals were not kept in reserves but ranged freely. It was therefore necessary for the sons of such settlers to learn to ride and shoot from an early age. The Boers were organised into local commandos that trained together and which could be called upon in time of conflict. In some ways it was similar to how local people kept themselves at the ready in medieval England or indeed frontier America. The Boers knew every kopje from which to attack and every kloof (chasm) in which to hide, ready for passing British units. Their overwhelming advantage was that as most were farmers they could retreat to their farms for food and rest; they could store their weapons there and the farms provided a place for commandoes to meet and plan their strategy.

After June 1900 there were many engagements with the Boers but they could not really be called battles, rather skirmishes on the open veldt or encounters when the Boers ambushed unsuspecting British soldiers. In 1901 more soldiers had to be recruited through the Imperial Yeomanry. This second group were recruited with a financial incentive and many more working-class men with families joined up. Another incentive was the promise of land in South Africa after victory. This group was poorly trained compared to the earlier recruitment and men had to be sent back either because they were medically or otherwise unfit to serve. It was the realisation of the state of health of many working-class recruits that led to army reforms after the war. Indeed this inspired some of the social reforms of the 1906 Liberal Government such as the provision of school milk and school dinners.

When Lord Kitchener took command in November 1900 he decided that a new strategy had to be adopted against the enemy. He reasoned that if the commandos could go back to their farms to keep themselves replenished, then those farms had to be destroyed. Initially the British had set up refugee camps for some women and older men to escape the fighting. Refugee implies someone fleeing to a place of safety but very soon these camps were used for women and children evicted from their farms which would then be destroyed either by fire or by dynamite. The policy had started under Lord Roberts but then was usually in reprisal for an attack on British troops. Under Kitchener, however, the policy became systematic. The destruction was completed by killing all the livestock on the farm. Not only was this wanton destruction of food but as the carcasses of animals were left to rot in the open water courses became polluted. Initially the families were simply left in the open after their farms were destroyed but increasingly this 'Scorched Earth' policy saw families being taken from their farms and transported to the camps, now known as concentration camps. The women and their children had no choice in the matter. These camps used tented accommodation and looked like army encampments set up on the veldt, which provided little in the way of shelter from the elements. The tents were frequently overcrowded and let in the rain. Most people had to sleep on the bare earth. The rations were meagre and in the early days the authorities deliberately imposed half rations on families where the husbands were still fighting, the idea being that somehow the wife would persuade the husband to surrender. In the meantime the children suffered. In any event there was never enough food to go round and fresh produce was unheard of. The conditions were unhygienic and the polluted water had the same effect as it did on the British soldiers. Boer families on the veldt lived a fairly isolated life providing their own food and having minimal contact with others. Taken away from this existence their resistance to disease was low and the young children were particularly vulnerable. Measles was the real killer and spread rapidly The South African winter of June 1901 was one of the harshest on the record, with snow falling on the veldt.[1] The combined effect of all these things on the young children proved devastating. Every day there were processions of coffins, usually for the little ones, being taken to the cemetery.

At the same time, Kitchener began building a system of blockhouses to trap Boer commandoes. These blockhouses were akin to small forts that could be manned by a small number of soldiers and Kitchener had barbed wire laid between them to trap Boer fighters. Thomas Galley, the young man who left the carpet factory and joined up in Worcestershire, describes this stage of the war as going on 'drives' looking for Boers and driving them into the blockhouse lines.

The 'Scorched Earth' policy, the concentration camps and the building of blockhouses were the major elements of British strategy in the latter part of the war. Yet it is difficult to find written testimony about it from many soldiers. The policy was said to particularly unpopular with some of the earlier recruits to the Imperial Yeomanry who were educated men who left to become officers in regular army units or to become civil servants. It may be the case that because of their education they had the facility to move to more agreeable posts in this way whereas the ordinary Tommy had to stay with his unit and carry out orders.

There are photographs of farms being burnt or dynamited and Boer women can be seen watching outside with the few possessions they were allowed to retrieve. These photos are rarely attributed. There are two important pieces of testimony resulting from soldiers' interviews many years later. However, in contemporary diaries and letters there are just a few comments concerning this, for example by Charles Ireland, who was referred to in Chapter 4 describing death from enteric. In a letter to his old headmaster at the British Seaman's Orphanage on 1 December 1900 he says: 'For two months we have been marching about burning down farms and turning out the women and children. This might seem cruel, but what would the cowards do to our women if they had the chance?' Private Ireland seems caught in between the wisdom of his commanding officers and trying to justify what might seem a callous act to his old headteacher.[2]

In a film made for BBC in the 1960s the actor and film-maker Trevor Griffiths interviews a fellow Welshman, then in his late seventies, who describes having to evict women and children from their homes prior to burning them. His face is a picture of misery as he says: 'It was horrible' and when asked why he did it he says with a look of despair 'Orders, that's why'. This gentleman also revealed a penny-pinching example of the army's treatment of the ordinary soldier. Most men at death were sewn into a blanket for burial. He described with real bitterness that the cost of this blanket was deducted from the man's final wages sent home to his wife.

Joseph Collet was an enlisted man serving with a Highland regiment, although he was from London. The account of his time in South Africa was recorded by Jenny Lee, a young nurse and midwife in the East End during the 1950s. She wrote a

The Bitter End

number of books which the BBC have serialised in as the *Call the Midwife* series. Joseph Collet was a patient who became her friend and the interviews provide a real insight into the lives of Eastenders, his time in the army and, in one chapter in particular, the Boer War. His account echoes so many of the experiences of other soldiers. He describes a horrific battle when, having climbed to the top of a hill, the soldiers realised that the Boer sharpshooters were on a higher hill and aiming straight at them. This could only have been at Spion Kop. He continues to talk about the death toll from enteric which he escaped but describes how he felt he had been spared for an even worse fate. As he recounts:

> Somehow I survived and had to take part in what was called the 'Bitter End'. After two and a half years of fighting we were no nearer to victory than we had been at the beginning. We couldn't engage the enemy. They were always hiding and attacking our lines, our communications, our stores, always surprising us. So our generals decided to attack their food supplies. This meant attacking their farms. A scorched earth policy was approved and we private soldiers had to carry it out. We hated it. Most of us felt degraded and emasculated, attacking women and children. We turned them out of their houses and burned their farms and barns. We killed their animals and burned their fields. Nothing was left after we finished. They were turned out to wander the veldt with no water, no food, prey to wild animals. I remember one young Boer woman with two little children and a baby. She was sobbing, begging us to spare her. I wanted to but refusal to obey military orders is unthinkable. It would have meant execution by firing squad if I had done so. Perhaps I would have risked it if I were single. But my money was going to Sally and the boys and to my mother for the rent. What could I do? And even if I

had disobeyed orders, it would have done no good. Other men would have carried out the job.

'He looked very grim and bitter' was how Jenny Lee described him.

'It was humiliating to us and our commanding officers. We were sent out to fight men, not defenceless women and children. We should never have done it. Never.' Jennifer worth describes how Mr Collet clenched his hands tightly at this point during the interview.

'It was a black time for the British Empire. Thirty thousand women and children died. Mostly young children and we were disgraced in the eyes of the world. We outnumbered the Boer fighting men by twenty-five to one, yet even then we couldn't win without attacking their homes, their women folk and their children. In the spring of 1903 I sailed for home and I was discharged from the army in 1906.'[3]

Thomas Stones' sister Deborah refers to him giving food to Boer women and children. That simple humanity is often a feature of war; there is no doubt that seeing hungry children looking just like the children that he knew back home would have touched his conscience. Deborah knew that by telling her this that her brother risked punishment and she warns him to be careful. Thomas also refers to the blockhouse lines being established to ensnare the Boers.

The camps were erected across a wide area of the country with a particular concentration along the railway lines but some were as far south as Cape Town and at least one was in Pretoria. In all there were some fifty camps set up for the white Boer families. As well as these camps there were also many set up for black people where they were expected to grow their own food, some of which could be requisitioned for the army. If anything, the conditions in the black camps were harsher than those in the white ones. No food was provided as they were expected to

The Bitter End

provide for themselves and even tents were denied them. Building their own shelters from anything available was hard and such structures would have been particularly vulnerable in the bitter winter of 1901. In both sets of camps death from disease and hunger was rife. Amongst the Boers 27,000 people died and of those 23,000 were young children. No record was kept of the deaths of black people, a terrible indictment of the fact that they were seen as expendable, if indeed considered human at all. A conservative estimate made in recent years says there were at least 14,000 deaths. Military records at the National Army Museum in London refer to a black 'refugee camp' on the banks of the Modder River where bodies from the camp were polluting the water. Recent excavations on a farm at Alleman railway siding near Brandfort in the Free State uncovered 653 graves of black people in what had been a Boer War concentration camp. But their names will never be known.

As a consequence of the change in British policy families were being driven off their land and now forced to live in camps on the veldt where their children died because they could no longer be looked after properly. The fact that this suffering went unacknowledged by the British state and then was hidden from ordinary British people left a deep and bitter legacy amongst the Boers. News of the harsh conditions in the camps was brought back to England by a lady called Emily Hobhouse. This was the same person cited in Chapter 4 who had spoken out against the war at a meeting in Liskeard. She was a vicar's daughter from Cornwall who had already travelled to Minnesota, America to undertake welfare work with Cornish miners. She was delegated to the task by her uncle Leonard Courtney, a Liberal MP, and arrived in South Africa in September 1900. She travelled to Bloemfontein and was horrified at the conditions. She found families sleeping on bare earth and existing on a poor diet as well as having to use polluted water and lacking even basic hygiene such as soap.[4]

She also travelled to Springfontein, approximately seventy miles to the south, where she saw piteous sights, particularly amongst the children. In present-day Springfontein a large memorial to the victims of the camps stands alongside a cemetery for British soldiers. Here too are the graves of those from the Welsh Hospital whose story is in Chapter 4. Poignantly, on the outside of this town, lies a small cemetery recording the deaths of thirty-six unbaptised babies believed to have been born to Boer women from the concentration camps and fathered by British soldiers.

In that last year of the war the Imperial Yeomanry constituted a growing part of the British offensive. This second recruitment was, as we have seen, encouraged by the financial incentive of five shillings a week and the lure of land in South Africa after the war. Not surprisingly the army managed to recruit largely amongst working-class men who were either jobless or needed better pay for themselves and their dependents. Many of these new recruits were dispatched into probably the most difficult situations of the war which involved fighting the Boer commandoes on the open veldt, manning the blockhouses and burning the farms thus bringing the families into the camps. In their first engagement at Vlakfontein in May 1901 they fled after suffering seventy casualties leaving other units, the Derbyshires and the artillery, to be gunned down.

In a skirmish near Rustenburg there was some improvement and they acquitted themselves well. Undoubtedly their worst disaster occurred at the Battle of Groenkop. Sometimes referred to as the Battle of Tweefontein, named after a nearby farm, this action was less a battle than an attack on sleeping soldiers. Poignantly it took place in the early hours of Christmas Day near a town called Bethlehem. Clearly the British army officers had not learnt the dangers of warfare in and around the South African terrain as evidenced by the battles of Spion Kop and Magersfontein. The British soldiers were led to the top of

The Bitter End

Groenkop on Christmas Eve and, feeling secure, they celebrated with rum and plum pudding. They clearly believed their position to be impregnable. However, no one had been sent to reconnoitre the hill and the sentry on duty was in the wrong position. In stark contrast the legendary Boer commander Christian De Wet had scouted the camp in the days beforehand and had found that there was a gulley up the side of the hill at Groenkop which his troops could climb easily under cover of darkness. The soldiers' camp promised rich pickings for his commandos, who by this time were short of food and ill-clothed. A British soldier reported later than one Boer soldier was wearing a Boer 'vrouw's' dark dress and bonnet. When they reconnoitred and discovered safe passage to the top of the hill, the Boers also found out that there was food, drink, horses, weapons and ammunition. So it happened that around three in the morning of Christmas Day the Boer forces stealthily climbed up the gully and stormed the sleeping British encampment. Men rose to defend the camp but they were at a clear disadvantage having risen bleary-eyed from the night before. One young officer, Lieutenant Jack Watney, tried to lead a charge but was gunned down. Men around him said it was futile but this nineteen-year-old man typified the attitude of his class. His intention was noble but any chance of success was slight. Young Watney had been an heir to the well-known beer fortune. At least fifty-seven British men died that morning, which did not include the number of native soldiers who again were not recorded. A local doctor, Geoffrey Reid, from Bethlehem, also lost his life that fateful day.

One of the casualties that night was a young man called **Hubert Akehurst**. Aged just twenty-four, Hubert was an ex-pupil of Brighton Grammar School. They recorded his death with deep regret and cited the *Sussex Daily News*:

> It is barely a year since Hubert Akehurst went out to war as a volunteer in the 53rd Company of the Imperial Yeomanry.

A letter received from him a few days before Christmas mentioned the fact that he was located at this camp, and was expecting to spend Christmas there. When news came of the daring storming of the camp by the Boers and our heavy losses his family were overwhelmed with the keenest anxiety which culminated in the painful shock of seeing his name under the heading so terrible in its significant brevity 'Killed'. He was only twenty four years old, tall, broad-shouldered and a favourite with all who knew him. His death in the prime of youth has come as a great shock to his friends, as well as the father, mother and family to whom the horrors of war are thus brought so painfully home. A pathetic incident is that a letter from the young soldier reached a friend the day after his death was published. In the last letter his parents received he mentions with pleasurable anticipation how he is looking forward to a happy Christmas. They had got a piano in camp, and a good singer and expected a lively time.

Young **Alfred Whitby**, from London, who had been in the Yeomanry since the first recruitment wrote to his mother on Boxing Day. 'No doubt you will have heard of the disaster that befell the Yeomanry.' The letter is sent from Elands River which was only a short distance from Groenkop. He said he was sending it 'with speed' so his parents would be reassured he was safe. It shows how quickly the news of such disasters reached home at this point in the war. The disaster that befell the Yeomanry at Groenkop was probably the worst defeat in this latter part of the war and the casualties were mainly poorly-trained volunteers. That it happened on Christmas Day was indeed poignant but the practice in the early part of the war to desist from fighting on Sundays and religious holidays had long fallen by the wayside. With their women and children in concentration camps the Boers were no longer willing to pay attention to these niceties. A lack

The Bitter End

of foresight and planning by the British command directly lead to these deaths.

At Yserspruit and later Tweebosch, units largely consisting of Imperial Yeomanry suffered defeats. Tweebosch was a heavy defeat. Two thousand Boers attacked with artillery and the colonial and yeomanry troops fled leaving the regular troops overwhelmed. Led by Colonel Methuen, whose troops had been overwhelmed at Magersfontein, they lost sixty-eight men killed, 121 wounded and 600 taken prisoner.

Despite some later victories for the Boers, they had become dispirited. Their wives and families were in the camps and they had lost children, their farms were despoiled and they were exhausted. Many of them had been taken prisoner and sent to British colonies far away such as Ceylon and Bermuda. They had a desire to return to normal life, to rebuild their farms and raise their crops. In essence this is why the Boers eventually sued for peace.

Peace was concluded by the Treaty of Vereeniging which was signed between the Boers and British command on 31 May 1902. The British were the victors but that victory came at a terrible cost. Twenty-two thousand British lives alone were lost. In South Africa an enormous amount of rebuilding of farms and some whole towns needed to take place. The cost to the British exchequer was around £210 million, the equivalent of £5.7 billion today; so much that it is said that proposed reforms of old-age pensions had to be deferred for almost a decade.

This peace treaty was signed between the two belligerent parties, the British and the Boers. The black people, who constituted the majority of the population in South Africa, had no involvement in the process. When the parties met again in 1906 a motion to give black and coloured people the franchise was rejected, the British opting to pander to the wishes of their previous enemies in this matter. This refusal to give black peoples any civil rights continued and from 1948 became part of the nascent apartheid regime which was enshrined in the constitution when South Africa left the Commonwealth in 1961. Many historians would now argue that the treatment of their own families in the concentration camps and its lack of acknowledgement in the outside world left many Boers bitter. Those men who fought to the very end were known by that name 'the bittereinders', literally the bitter enders and it is from among that group that the men who would create the apartheid system arose.

Chapter 8

'A LAND FIT FOR HEROES'?

When the war ended in May 1902 many men were able to start the journey home they'd been looking forward to so much, but so many men being demobilised at once sometimes meant considerable waits in camps at least a few miles from the main departure ports of Durban and Cape Town. Officers ordered that they should not be too near the temptations of either of those cities!

The soldiers returned to many large and well-orchestrated official welcomes in towns and villages across the country. In Dundee, which had lost so many men at the early battles of Magersfontein and Paardeberg, there was a lavish homecoming. The soldiers, who had already been feted in Perth, travelled to their home town of Dundee by train. They were greeted first by the Lord Provost of Dundee, who welcomed them to the city.

> Under the direction of their officers they fell in on the east end of the platform. In full public view they came in for a great ovation. The vast crowd cheered wildly, thousands of mill lassies broke out into the vociferous singing of 'Soldiers of the Queen,' many of them accompanying the refrain by waving improvised flags of brightly-coloured material. Then there was an awkward pause. Some little delay occurred in forming up the order of procession, but the crowd made good use of the time in shouting friendly greetings to the lads in khaki, and the officers were afforded an opportunity

of exchanging greetings with their friends. At length the volunteers were accommodated in the vehicles in waiting for them, and to the accompaniment of deafening cheers the procession began its march citywards.

The Lord Provost's speech was profuse in praise of the troops and this was echoed by the crowd with spontaneous cheers for the soldiers and the king.

Formal celebrations continued with the dignitaries but eventually the troops were released to their families and friends.

Directly the word 'Dismiss' was given the active service men were surrounded and borne off by their volunteer comrades, who triumphantly escorted them outside the iron gates. As each bronzed 'kiltie' passed out to the street he was pounced upon by anxious relatives and friends he had not seen for many a day. The crowd awarded them all a deafening ovation. Dozens of spectators gathered round to have the honour of shaking hands with the men and giving them a congratulatory pat on the back. Especially warm was the greeting given by the crowd to Lieutenant Harry Smith, as looking in the best of health and spirits he made his appearance outside the gates. He is evidently as popular with the crowd as with his own soldiers, and the cordiality of his welcome back was fully appreciated by him. The night must have been a great one in the respective family circles of the returned heroes, and doubtless it was well into the small hours of the morning before the most sensational stories of life on the veldt had been recounted.[1]

This ceremony was a celebration but it also reflected the relief of the population to see their men back home. For the relatives of the many who died at Elandslaagte, Modder River, Paardeberg and particularly Magersfontein, the occasion would

'A Land Fit for Heroes'?

have been tainted with sadness for the loved ones they would never see again.

Homecoming ceremonies took place across the country all with appropriate enthusiasm and maintained with set protocols. Reports listed the important people of each town and paid tribute to returning soldiers. In places as far apart as Totnes in Devon, Staffordshire and Lancashire all of whom had contributed massively to the war, there were scenes of wild jubilation.

In the small Peak District town of Wirksworth in Derbyshire a great show was mounted. The local paper headlined: 'Wirksworth and the Returned Warriors, An important function. Public Presentations. A glorious event. The Town en Fete. Honouring the killed.' A platform was erected in the main square for three in the afternoon and people were given the rest of the day off from work. The proceedings were led by Captain Pole Gell of the 2nd Battalion Coldstream Guards who had been greeted at the station by a large crowd welcoming home this local warrior. Flags were out and Chinese lanterns had been lit in many windows. He made a speech saying how glad he was to be home and thanking people for their kindness in sending out so many parcels to him and his men. Then he was roundly cheered and the National Anthem was sung, after which local people and the tenants of Hopton Hall accompanied him home to the Hall with the band again playing 'God Save the King'.[2]

For the returning troops those ceremonies were uplifting, combining a mixture of relief, jubilation and pure pleasure at seeing their home towns and their families again. But when the excitement died down each soldier and his family had to take stock and see what life back home had to offer. The war had spanned two centuries and two monarchs. Queen Victoria had died in 1901 after a reign of sixty-three years. Her son, Edward, who succeeded her, reigned for just ten years although the term 'Edwardian' has been used to describe not just his reign but the epoch leading up to 1914 when war broke out again. During this period the strict morality characteristic of his mother's era was superseded. Though married to Alexandra, Edward openly consorted with mistresses and those in his circle emulated his behaviour. Some members of the educated upper middle classes embraced alternative life styles as well. The Bloomsbury Group comprised of former Cambridge men and women who pursued the creative arts and eschewed monogamous relationships. The children's author, Edith Nesbit, for example, shared a household with her husband, another woman, their housekeeper and their children. All of these groups had sufficient money to support such lifestyles. For the ordinary soldiers who returned in 1902 life remained much the same as the one they had left and being able to support themselves and their families was the main priority.

The census returns of many of our soldiers show them to be labourers or mill hands, if indeed they were lucky enough to have work. Their wives and sweethearts are usually general servants or charwomen. In places that had provided so many young men for the conflict in South Africa the conditions were poor. In Lancashire, from where so many of those who had fought at Spion Kop came, the cotton industry was subject to the economic cycles of boom and bust. **Thomas Stones'** relatives and friends had maintained a lively correspondence with him throughout his time with the Lancashire Fusiliers in South Africa. In September 1901, whilst suggesting the war would be over soon, a letter from his brother-in-law, Jimmy Cronshaw referred to the numbers of wounded soldiers attending a Blackburn Rovers' match. He said 'Blackburn is full of them now'. A month earlier Jimmy had written: 'There will be no going away on holiday as the mills are doing badly at present on account of the Chinese crisis. Several mills in my neighbourhood are being stopped altogether.' Later they try to reassure him that they will do their best to make him comfortable when he returns from the war. They caution that: 'The trade of the town is not very rosy at present but it is better than last August and September.' Jimmy is employed at the local

'A Land Fit for Heroes'?

workhouse and tells him that they were getting some very bad cases: 'Everyone seems to be going mad here.'[3]

The Salvation Army, which had been at work in South Africa itself, worked amongst the urban poor at home. In an article entitled 'Silent Looms' written in 1902 they describe the devastation caused in Lancashire by the slump in the cotton trade. 'Some people were living on part time work, some on none.' The article recounts that people there were frugal and used to keeping money aside for hard times but that this present slump was straining those resources beyond endurance. One of their own 'Soldiers' had been out of work for twelve months and could find none. A young woman with no family to support her had been turned away from receiving help until the following week. One article under the title 'The Starving Poor' also describes the freezing conditions in London that winter, exhorting its readers to contribute to the poor and destitute whilst they enjoy their warm homes.

Benjamin Seebohm Rowntree had carried out an in-depth study on poverty in York in 1899 with the results published in 1901. With assistants he visited 11,560 families and he calculated the amount of money people needed for food, fuel, light, rent and basic personal items. If they had insufficient for the whole family they fell below the poverty line and he revealed that in York approximately 28 per cent of the population fell below it. These findings corresponded with those of Charles Booth in London who mapped the city according to levels of poverty or wellbeing. Rowntree's findings challenged the view that poverty only existed in the capital. York and the county of Yorkshire had sent many men to the war. The large memorial opposite the Minster records the deaths of over a thousand men. Many would have been from the city and many had families who would now have to struggle on without their male breadwinners.

Jack London, a contemporary American writer, famous for *White Fang* and *The Call of the Wild*, described the life of the East

End of London in his non-fiction work *The People of the Abyss* published in 1903. He wrote this first-hand account whilst living in Whitechapel for several months, sometimes staying in workhouses or sleeping on the streets. The conditions he experienced and wrote about were the same as those endured by an estimated 500,000 of the contemporary London poor.

The countryside had suffered badly from a long agricultural depression in late Victorian times and by 1901 the male workforce was reduced by a third. Many soldiers who had been agricultural labourers before the war returned to find their jobs had disappeared. This depression had led to high levels of emigration throughout the last years of the nineteenth century. J. B. Priestley wrote in *The Edwardians* that: 'Most of these years working people were rather worse off than they had been in the later years of the previous century as prices were higher and wages had not increased.'

In researching this book soldiers' relatives provided stories from the war and many had inherited medals. Some were able to say what the men did on their arrival home. However, it must be remembered that there are no living soldiers from this war. The accounts that have kindly been given to me are from their grandchildren or indeed their great-grandchildren. Finding the stories of those who slipped through the net was much more challenging for a variety of reasons. The stories of people struggling, or worse still finding themselves in the workhouse, might well be considered shameful. Therefore not many such stories have passed down the generations. Many women widowed through the conflict rapidly remarried through fear of having no support for themselves and their children. This becomes clear when looking at the records of the Transvaal Widows' Fund, which was set up to aid war widows.

In the early stages of the war there was great sympathy for the soldiers and their families and many people had given to charities. These funds were largely held locally and therefore no uniformity was maintained. In view of the enormity of the demand for charitable beneficence such local charities could not hope to keep up with the needs of disabled soldiers and bereaved families. Essentially charities existed to make grants for special needs and could not provide a weekly income. If relatives could not help with support, and most were from families of moderate means, then recourse to the Poor Law and the workhouse was the only option. An article in a 1903 newspaper reported that 'so many soldiers were applying for poor relief that the War Office directed them to re-enlist with reserves if they possessed a valid certificate to do so'. A cartoon at the time shows a soldier with an amputated leg following a sign pointing to the workhouse.

By 1906 questions were being asked in the House of Commons about disabled servicemen living in the workhouses as for example the following exchange recorded in *Hansard*:

> Mr Claude Hay (Shoreditch, Hoxton): I beg to ask the Secretary of State for War whether he will state the number of soldiers now in workhouses who were discharged from military hospitals suffering from incurable illness contracted while serving His Majesty; whether the pensions to which these soldiers are entitled are in whole or in part are retained by the guardians of the workhouse of which the soldiers are now inmates and whether they are treated in every respect as regards clothes, food, discipline or any money they may receive other than their pensions.
>
> Mr Haldane: The number is not known in the Department. Secondly the Guardians have the same claim on any pensions these men may be entitled to, as upon any other pensions. The general treatment of inmates of workhouses does not come within the purview of my department; but it is known that in some cases old soldiers are allowed to retain some portion of their pension for the purchase of small luxuries such as tobacco.

The Minister of War seemed to find it easy to abrogate responsibility for soldiers injured in South Africa.[4]

The slump in the cotton industry produced a widespread recession in Lancashire about which the Salvation Army wrote. Looms lay idle and people were without work. They queued at mobile soup kitchens set up by charities as the only way to help whole families avoid starvation. No doubt the relatives of men who had fought in the war were amongst them; a sad contrast with the African population of Mafeking who had had to endure the same ordeal just two or three years before.

Unemployment was not just a problem in the north and with no benefits payable to those out of work it caused great hardship. This affected many soldiers returning from the war. In 1903 in Exeter the local newspaper commented on the number of unemployed reservists and criticised employers who seemed unwilling to take them on. In Hackney in east London the newly-formed Trades Council mounted a campaign to bring attention to the large scale of unemployment. The war had ended in 1902 and hundreds of demobbed soldiers came home to find their jobs filled by others and there was little chance of finding alternative work. Walter Southgate, an original Social Democratic Federation (SDF) member of the Trades Council, said: 'Many parts of London were badly hit and the Labour Movement began a long and protracted agitation. The prime minister, Balfour refused to meet our delegation on several occasions and Keir Hardie, the first Labour MP, was similarly refused leave to introduce a motion into Parliament.' Then in December of that year a National Unemployed Committee was set up to coordinate the action and local committees were encouraged. On 21 December an invitation was issued for a conference in Hackney involving Trade Unions, Labour, Temperance and working-class organisations 'to consider ways of coping with the situation locally'. In the following February men from Hackney joined in demonstrations through the West End culminating in a huge demonstration in Trafalgar Square.

'A Land Fit for Heroes'?

Local demonstrations followed, including one through the well-off part of Hackney where the demonstrators dressed up and banged a kettledrum and played a bugle. Walter Southgate said: 'We wanted to stir up the middle classes. But this and the other marches fell on deaf ears and often the reason for continuing the marches was to keep up morale.' The unemployment problem grew worse and by 1904 several London Poor Law Unions were making arrangements to increase their casual ward accommodation. In Hackney the Board of Guardians supported a resolution containing a list of proposals for tackling the problem which included the establishment of labour colonies, an eight-hour day and the undertaking of public works which would provide employment. The Trades Council wrote to the Secretary of the Local Government Board calling for public works to dredge the Thames and reclaim the foreshore 'as a palliative for the current distress'. The government watched and listened in stony silence and nothing was done. There was a huge rally in Trafalgar Square on 9 July 1905. In September Hackney representative Alfred Payne attended a meeting at which the London Central Workers Committee was formed. Local campaigning continued and although the government chose to ignore the issue it made an impression, with the *Daily Graphic* commenting that the public now could not ignore the issues.

As a direct way to alleviate need, a breakfast fund was organised for local children. Originally for children of trade unionists it was extended to meet the needs of more children as the fund increased. A concert was used to raise money and local coffee shops were visited to see if they would cater for local children. The scheme was so successful that at one stage 500 children were being fed each week. The scale of the organisation and campaigning in Hackney reflect the scale of the problem in a world with no Labour exchanges or unemployment benefit to tide workless men over.[5]

Some soldiers returning from the war experienced hardship;

for some the trauma of active service had other consequences. The case of **James Homeyard** from Exeter is a sorry tale of an ex-soldier. James had been in the regular army serving for some ten years before going to fight in South Africa. He was known in Exeter and had sometime been a cabman at Exeter St David's station. On returning home he could not find work and took up the offer of his former commanding officer, Sir Robert Ward, to stay at his residence in London where he attempted to look for work. We do not know what happened in the intervening time but after eight months James took himself up on Hampstead Heath one morning and shot himself through the head.

A newspaper reported;

Dr G. Danford Thomas held an inquest yesterday at Hampstead Dispensary on James Homeyard, aged 31, an ex-soldier in the Seventh Dragoon Guards who served during the South African War and was found dead on Hampstead Heath on Sunday morning from the effects of a revolver shot. According to mother of the deceased her son returned from South Africa in June 1902 and took part with his regiment in the King's coronation procession. He left Exeter for London in search of work which he failed to find and chafed under his enforced idleness. The Honourable Robert Ward, brother of the Earl of Dudley and the deceased's former officer had maintained her son in London and had done his best to secure him employment. The deceased grieved to be a burden to anyone. PC Carr said that he had found him lying dead in some bushes near Pooley Farm, North End, Hampstead Heath. Beside him was a six-chambered revolver and there was an open letter. It read 'I have not up to now received my medals which were hardly won. My most sincere regret for the trouble I have caused to the Honourable Robert Ward to say nothing of the considerable expense which I hope to cut short before the night is over for which I hope he will forgive me. I came to London eight months ago quite willing to work for my living and I have not done anything since and I don't see any prospects of getting anything. I have been thinking of this way out for some time.' The verdict given was suicide while of unsound mind.

The following day the Registrar for Hampstead sent his death certificate to the War Office requesting the usual fee of 2/6 plus stamp duty. If James, who had the support of the Honourable Robert Ward, previously a Conservative MP and brother of an Earl, still had problems then the difficulties for other ex-soldiers can only be imagined.

Work on stress related to war was not well advanced then. However the way in which James was affected may be inferred from a poem he wrote whilst in Johannesburg in November 1900. It is dedicated to his close friend and comrade Jim who died out there.

Comrade Jim, a story of a battle in South Africa

War-war! What is it? You talk in a mighty way,
As if you know all about it, when you've read what the papers say.
A thrill of delight runs through you when you hear of a victory won
And at the brave deeds of our soldiers you utter a proud 'Well done.'

You sit in a cosy parlour, surrounded by children and wife,
You smile at the growing picture that makes you so happy in life;
But what about the red coats fighting away on the foam
And what about the children and the heart broken wife at home?

> War-war! What is it? Its horrors you cannot know
> Until you have been in the carnage in front of a terrible foe;
> Where the bullets are flying and whizzing and flowing about like rain,
> And you hear the roar of the cannon booming loudly over the plains.
>
> And the cries of the dying and wounded are mixed in the awful din.
> And at the sight of your comrades falling you set your teeth close and grin.
> Then when the battle is over and the field of blood you walk
> But there you are safe in England, where it's easy enough to talk.

These are the first four impassioned verses of his poem. The battle he refers to at the beginning is the one where his best friend 'Comrade Jim' of the title died. He describes Jim's death and his sorrow in detail and ends by saying he wants an end to the jingo spirit and invokes 'Jehovah' bringing peace. James's message is clear, he is sick of the war and of those at home who are cheerleaders for the war whilst knowing nothing of its horrors.

James's poem is expressed in the style and metre of late Victorian times but the sentiments would fit well with the outpouring of anti-war verse penned in the First World War. His grief about his lost friend and the anger he felt at the glorification of war were likely compounded when he himself could not find work back in England.

Nowadays it is almost commonplace to talk of Post-Traumatic Stress Disorder when considering the problems of servicemen returning from conflicts. There was no such knowledge during the Boer War and many men may have returned home with broken spirits and without any support. There was some sympathy for James Homeyard but no real understanding of how the loss of his comrade and what he had witnessed would have disturbed him. The Suicide Act which allowed for unsuccessful suicides to be prosecuted, and indeed imprisoned, was not repealed until 1961 and this influenced public attitudes.

There were recognised physical symptoms attributed to military conflict at the time of the war. One was Disordered Action of the Heart, believed to result from the pressure of webbing when carrying heavy equipment over long distances. The weight was believed to have caused constriction of the blood vessels forcing the blood vessels to pump excessively to maintain circulation. This was recognised earlier both in the Crimean and American Civil War but it became a major cause of invalidity during the Boer War. Official statistics show 3,631 servicemen were hospitalised with the condition and of these 41 per cent were invalided home. There they were generally discharged since there was no known way of treating it. Military physicians continued to work on ways of preventing future cases. In South Africa some of the highest incidences were amongst the RAMC who had to cover vast distances carrying heavy equipment. In the latter stages of the war when the British maintained mobile forces covering large distances on the veldt against Boer guerrillas the RAMC were under greater pressure keeping up with the columns.[6]

During this war rheumatism or muscle and joint pain associated with fatigue became a prominent cause of invalidity. In Chapter 3 Colonel Mary Murray had noted this during the campaign to relieve Ladysmith. She saw young men who, a few weeks before, had been alive and vigorous laid low by pain and exhaustion which she attributed to them sleeping on cold wet ground. In the same chapter we saw eighteen-year-old Denis Devine who died of exposure in a pool of cold water overnight. Anthony Bowlby, a civilian surgeon who had worked at hospitals in Rondebosch and Bloemfontein during 1900 noted pain in the form of headache, generally posterior, pains in the neck, pains in the back and the limbs so cases are generally sent back as cases of rheumatism; general feebleness of the muscular system amounting to paralysis more or less pronounced.[7] These figures show clearly that apart from those killed or wounded, morbidity was high in this conflict and that these illnesses were largely the result of the conditions experienced by the soldiers.

Reading Dr Frederick Treves's account of some of the gross injuries which soldiers received at the battles to relieve Ladysmith it is likely that many would have come home to be treated in military hospitals such as Netley in Hampshire. Many would have been confined to their own homes unable to work. Occupational therapy was in its infancy then so little help would have available. Thomas Stones' brother-in-law had commented in 1901 that Blackburn was full of disabled soldiers, yet so few individual accounts survive. These men had fought for their country but their lot was soon forgotten. Accounts that survived are for men whose injuries were particularly gross and who came to the attention of important people and were reported in the press.

There were pensions for soldiers incapacitated by wounds or injuries received in action or in performance of their military duties:

- NCOs and men wholly disabled from 1/6 to 3/6 per day and for those partially disabled from 6d to 3s a day.
- NCOs and men disabled by sickness attributable service to receive pensions ranging from 6d to 1/6 a day.[8]

The level of disability was assessed by the Commissioners of Chelsea Hospital in accordance with circumstances. This kind of pension was not payable to volunteers and it was only paid to the disabled soldier; no mention is made of extra monies for the wife or children. It did not include money for extras necessitated by the disability e.g. wheelchairs, special boots or clothes.

Patrick Kelly, referred to in Chapter 3, received gross wounds

'A Land Fit for Heroes'?

at Spion Kop. He had survived two nights on the hill after the battle, an amazing feat since the high daytime temperatures would have plummeted once the sun went down. His arm was nearly severed and he had kept it from falling in amongst the bodies that littered the ground by holding his shirtsleeve between his teeth. He kept alive by drinking from any water bottles left by dead soldiers, a traumatic experience. When he was brought down and Dr Treves operated he was forced by that time to amputate both arms right up to the shoulder blades.

At home he was feted by Princess, later Queen, Alexandra, who gave him a silver pipe. The Royal Family offered him a place on the Sandringham estate but he preferred to stay at home in Burnley with his parents. He was given the freedom of Bury and other awards. His miraculous recovery after treatment in South Africa by Treves enabled him some time in his own home town but ultimately the effect of his injuries proved too much and in September 1905 after just a few days in bed he died of 'phitis' (the contemporary name for a type of tuberculosis) brought on by pneumonia, aged thirty-five. He received a military funeral and the nature of his injuries and the stoicism with which he bore them are remembered to this day. The Lancashire Fusiliers' Museum have a whole showcase devoted to him.

Sergeant James Boseley was severely injured at the Battle of Wagon Hill on 6 January 1900. A violent and chaotic battle that was made worse by being fought at night, it was one of the many fought during the campaign to relieve Ladysmith. We do not have the record but it is likely that he was operated on by Sir Frederick Treves who performed a double amputation on the left-hand side. It is unlikely that there was any other surgeon capable of this in the theatre of war at the time. James was said to be the first man to have survived such a procedure and to have been operated on in a field hospital with no antibiotics or access to blood transfusions meant his survival was nothing short of a miracle. James was feted when he arrived home at Southampton in April

1900 and after further recuperation was taken to visit his mother in Maidstone where crowds gathered to give him a hearty cheer. It was reported that he said his main regret was he could no longer serve the Queen as a soldier. By the time of the 1901 census he had been given a job as lodge keeper at Cranwells near Bath and was living alone there. However, soon after he married Sarah Ann Summers. Remarkably, they had four children born between 1902 and 1907. In 1911 they were living at the Royal Artillery Cottages, Claverton Down, Bath, which was one of the cottage homes established for wounded soldiers. He was then listed as an army pensioner. He died in 1915 of an acute intestinal obstruction. His survival into his forties and his fathering of four children are quite remarkable given the extent of his injuries.

Charles Webber of the Devonshire Regiment, as with James Boseley, was also severely wounded at Wagon Hill. A dum-dum bullet shattered his knee and as a result the limb was amputated well above the knee. The *Totnes Times* took up his case reporting that on arrival home he had received no money for three weeks and had been told he would receive just 1s 6d a week for the following year. This is the lower figure which was payable to the severely injured and certainly seems inconsistent with the level of his disability. The paper pointed out that Private Webber was a regular soldier and had no trade from which to earn a living. It is interesting to see the campaigning attitude of the newspaper which said having no money for three weeks may be 'a small matter to officials in Pall Mall but a very considerable hardship for a man without any means'. It might be that Charles himself thought little of the pension they offered him because by the 1901 census he had managed to find himself a post as an insurance clerk, presumably a sedentary occupation. He had married Bessie Jago but sadly she died soon after and the next trace we have of Charles is in the 1911 census by which time he is living in Exeter with his second wife and two children. Interestingly he is listed as an army pensioner and is head of a boys' reformatory.

'A Land Fit for Heroes'?

Cottage homes served a lucky few injured in the conflict. The Bedfordshire Regiment had such homes endowed by the Duke of Bedfordshire at Cheshunt in Hertfordshire.[9] **Henry Goodwin** was one resident. A regular soldier who had enlisted back in 1885, he was in almost constant pain and had been discharged totally disabled on 9 January 1901. He had lost the use of his legs through blocking of the main veins in both legs which was the result of long marches after enteric fever. Thus we see that even when someone had survived the blight of enteric they could not always escape a long march and its effects. **Henry Cooper** was another resident who'd fought in South Africa. at the bitter battle of Paardeberg in January 1900. He had gunshot wounds in both the chest and arm but could still do light work.

There is nothing in the correspondence with **Thomas Stones** that suggested any major illness or injury and he was not invalided home.[10] In July and August 1901 he did spend some time in the General Hospital at Elandsfontein but on release he was able to continue with his duties. Sadly there is no record of his return home but no doubt initially he would have gone to join his sister, Deborah and her husband, Jimmy. The next news of him is on 27 March 1906 when, aged just twenty-eight, Thomas died of heart failure. The death certificate says 'Aortic Disease and acute dilatation of the right heart.' He had a job and was working as a railway porter in Burnley. It seems unfair that after three years in the heat and battle of South Africa and having survived the carnage of Spion Kop that Thomas should die like this in the prime of his life. It may, however, not have been a coincidence if we remember the preponderance of cases of Disordered Action of the Heart caused by long marches with heavy equipment. Thomas was involved in the final stages of the war having to be always mobile to keep up with the Boer guerrillas. This may have put a strain on his heart which caught up with him in the end.

Private Martin Nolan came home from South Africa fit and well but it is what happened on his return that is perhaps the most extraordinary story in this book. He was born in Birmingham in March 1868. He was the ninth of eleven children and the sixth son. At the time of his birth his father was doing quite well, running a business on the canal side which dealt in provisions for passing barges, of which many passed through the canal system at that time. Martin attended school and could read and write. On leaving school he worked as a labourer but looking for adventure and the open air he enlisted in the Royal Welsh Fusiliers which was based at Wrexham in North Wales. On 4 October 1889 he became Private Martin Nolan, No 2576, having been passed fit in mind and body by the Medical Officer. He did further training in Wales and on New Year's Day 1891 left, like so many soldiers at the time, for India where he spent five years, returning on June 1896.[11]

He was sent to South Africa in October 1899 at the beginning of the war. He fought under the command of General Sir Redvers Buller and his subordinates Warren, Hart, Long, Methuen and Gatacre during the first year of the war. This is not a book about military tactics but certainly there were many criticisms of strategy both during and after the war. The Scottish solider at Magersfontein had questioned why 'Tommy Atkins' was not told about the Boer trenches in which they were hiding. The sketch map at Spion Kop had wrongly estimated the height of the hill. These mistakes and others cost the lives of many men. Questions too were raised in Parliament about the conduct of the war. Private Nolan too had many criticisms but nevertheless had fought throughout and won medal clasps for the Relief of Ladysmith, Orange Free State, Tugela Heights and Cape Colony. In February 1900 he was posted missing presumed killed after a battle at Tugela but was later found wounded on the field of battle.

That December day in 1902 when he returned to Birmingham it was voicing these views that were to change his life forever. Detraining at Snow Hill station, kit bag flung over his shoulder he was looking forward to walking the short distance to his family

'A Land Fit for Heroes'?

home in Price Street. But the platform was awash with newspaper reporters keen to get the soldiers' views on the controversy that had been raised in Parliament and the press over the various generals' military tactics. When asked Private Nolan could not resist and said 'The generals should be like that Little Fat Queen Victoria, f——-g dead.' His words were overheard by a Military Policeman and he was immediately arrested and charged. He faced a court martial, where he was found guilty but being deemed unfit to plead and the word 'insane' was inserted on his discharge papers. Where his signature was required on the word 'lunatic' was inserted. His army career ended on 13 January 1903 when he was committed to the local Lunatic Asylum at Winston Green where he remained until his death in March 1953 aged eighty-five. This was after fourteen years serving in the regular army with no charges brought against him. At that time asylums across the country were full of people who once admitted who then stayed many years until their death. At Exminster Asylum which took people from across the county of Devon there were many such cases although most exhibited some level of 'mental illness'. Examples include William who'd had typhoid and once admitted to the asylum started hearing voices. He was admitted aged twenty-seven in 1905 and stayed till his death in 1950. Walter, a naval seaman was also admitted aged twenty-seven and died there aged fifty-nine. In his case it was said he couldn't communicate and the constable had found him trying to 'make a connection' with a pig. These sad cases and many like them across the country merited treatment but not lifelong incarceration. However, they differ markedly from that of Private Nolan. No doubt the army hierarchy would have to conceive a soldier mad for criticising the generals in the recently ended conflict; worse still he had 'badmouthed' the recently deceased queen who was so venerated. Martin Nolan had to be made an example of for fear that other lowly soldiers took up the criticism for what they and their comrades suffered in South Africa. In prison he could still be viewed as rational, if wrong. As a lunatic he would be deemed not responsible for his actions and therefore what he'd said was not valid.

In 1903 his sister wrote to the authorities asking about Martin's finances and was informed that on the instructions of the War Office his monies were to be retained until he was fully recovered, discharged and well enough to furnish a receipt. In 1911 his nephew enquired again and was told that the monies were being used to pay the Poor Law Guardians for his upkeep at the asylum! Earlier reports show that disabled soldiers in workhouses were required to pay from their disability pensions. Eventually he was transferred to the hospital wing at Winston Green and when his second cousins visited they reported he was too institutionalised to care. When his young nieces visited it seems that every other word was an expletive which evinced nervous giggles from the girls. Thanks to his nephew Thomas Nolan, who wrote to his old regiment, he had a proper funeral and was laid to rest next to his parents in Witton Cemetery, Birmingham. What a terrible life for a vigorous young man who fought for Britain but who dared criticise the powers that be using an unacceptable expletive about the Queen.[12]

Chapter 9

SUFFER LITTLE CHILDREN

The aftermath of the Crimean War saw the first recognition that some support should be given to the wives and families of soldiers who had been killed or wounded. The 1834 Poor Law had abolished outdoor relief, the idea being that people must support themselves through work and those who could or would not should only get help through the strict regime of the workhouse. However, the authorities did see the wives and children of those who had served their country as more deserving and many still were able to receive outdoor relief. Some soldiers' wives still found themselves in workhouses but the authorities tried to avoid this.

At this time some provision was made for soldiers' children and in the aftermath of that war a fund was launched to raise subscriptions for the widows and orphans. An extraordinary £1.5 million was raised of which £35,000 was used to build an orphanage for girls whose fathers had perished in the war. Originally named the Royal Patriotic Victoria Asylum for Girls, it was opened by Queen Victoria herself in 1856. A large gothic building, it stood on the edge of Wandsworth Common. From the beginning the girls admitted were not all orphans, many having a mother living. Modern ideas about keeping the family together did not prevail then and taking in one or two children was seen as a way of alleviating the family's poverty. Sadly the asylum did not have a good history. Girls had to pump all their own water from a ground supply. On admission their heads were shaved to prevent lice and they had to wash in cold water in the yard. Even when heating was installed in staff quarters the girls' area was left unheated.[1]

During the Boer War some children were still being supported as a result of their father's deaths in this way. In another military institution, the Royal Victoria School, these are some of the girls admitted:

- Emily Lillian Walker, born 9 September 1898. She had two brothers and one sister. Her father, Robert Walker had seen twelve years' service in the East Surrey Regiment and had died of erysipelas and chronic alcoholism on active service.
- Phyllis Gertrude Locker born 30 September 1898, an only child. Her father Private George Locker had served with 2nd North Staffs and died of enteric on 7 June 1900
- Grace Mary Loft born 20 May 1899. She was an only child. Her father. George Loft was in the Royal Lancs regiment and was one of the many who was killed in action on 24 January 1900 at Spion Kop.[2]

The Transvaal Widows' Fund, which was created as part of the Patriotic Fund, operated nationally but was struggling to fulfil its aims with the demand from so many bereaved families. In 1904 a new appeal was launched for money. One contributor to the fund was no less a person than King Edward VII who gave 200 guineas saying that he hoped that would encourage other donors'. After the death of his mother, Queen Victoria, as king he was responsible for the army and its part in the conflict. As Duke of Cornwall he had been the officer in charge of the Devon and Cornwall Light Infantry who contributed many soldiers to the war.[3]

The fund was established to help widows and children of the conflict. There is no record of how individual cases were decided but the following were its guidelines: 'Each case is carefully investigated by the committees of the corporation; overlapping is avoided, habits of thrift and self dependence in recipients of benefits are encouraged and the future welfare of the child is especially guarded by withholding allowances from parents who neglect their health or education.' The idea of avoiding overlapping benefits is sensible but withdrawing monies from mothers who are deemed to have neglected their children's education would undoubtedly affect the children themselves. The text is silent on the consequences of this. However, legislation governing applications for poor relief at the time dictated that parents who had to ask for poor relief more than three times lost custody of their children.

What is known is that widows who remarried were immediately debarred from receiving assistance and the fund's record book shows that many others were dismissed with comments such as 'Unworthy' or 'Dismissed' written alongside their name. Up until the 1890s certain regiments had kept a book listing punishments for soldiers' wives; these punitive attitudes seem to have lodged in the minds of those assessing the claims, at least in their apparent lack of compassion.[4] After the fund was relaunched in 1904 some concession was made towards widows who had remarried.

Elizabeth Candy, the widow of Sergeant Candy who died at Spion Kop, was left with three young girls to bring up. Mary aged six was the daughter of James's first wife followed by Alice, aged three, and Bertha, aged two. James had been well known in Darwen and there was great sympathy for the family. A fund was started by public subscription which had raised £14 7s 6d by 24 February 1900; precisely a month after the battle where James Candy had perished. Interestingly, a letter signed 'A sympathiser' and enclosing a cheque made the following point: 'As regards the widow surely they will be able to get the war office authorities to make some proper and adequate provision for a case like this. The Government allowance to Reservists' wives have I believe recently been raised very considerably in deference to strong representations that have been made on the subject and I see that Mr Balfour promised in the House of Commons last night that some provision should be made for the widows of soldiers killed. This national duty certainly ought not to be left to private charity.'

Elizabeth did make an application to the Transvaal Widows' Fund. The book does not record if and when she was paid but since there are no negative comments against her name it may be hoped that she received some help. Nevertheless by the time of the 1901 census, Elizabeth was, like so many in the area, working as a cotton weaver. Three of her siblings were living with her in Bury Street and they were also working as cotton weavers and her mother, a widow, was there listed as a Housekeeper Domestic. The children were young and the variety of relatives working shifts would have ensured there was always someone there.

Poor Elizabeth had another tragedy to bear when in December 1901 Martha and Bertha both died. These are the two girls that James Candy had mentioned in his last letter home to his wife. Mortality of children under five, particularly those from working-class backgrounds, was high in those days owing to poor nutrition and illnesses that had no treatment. How hard this must have been for Elizabeth can only be imagined and this would have been compounded in early 1907 when she gave birth to a son called William, father not known, who died in infancy. By the time of the 1911 census Elizabeth, then thirty-six was still working as a cotton weaver and sharing the terraced house in Bury Street with her mother, stepdaughter, her married sister, Grace Killeen, and members of Grace's family. Remarkably, though, Elizabeth herself lived to the age of seventy-one. Dying in 1945, she had outlived her husband, James by forty-five years.

George Ravenhill, VC, was born in February 1872 in the Nechells district of Birmingham, one of a large family living in this working-class area of the city. He joined the 2nd Battalion

Suffer Little Children

Royal Scots Fusiliers and when he left for South Africa in 1899 his wife Florence and baby daughter Lilly were living at Long Acre, Aston near to Nechells. At the Battle of Colenso George along with other men in his battalion were in charge of the guns. As a result of inaccurate British mapping they were pushed into a blind loop on the river. Under Colonel Long's command the guns had been pushed further forward than General Buller had commanded and as fighting broke out several men were killed. George was one of those who retrieved the guns under fire and it was for this he was awarded the VC; the only private to receive this at Colenso. Freddy Roberts, son of Field Marshal Roberts, lost his life there and received the VC posthumously. George was awarded the honour by the Duke of York in Pietermaritzburg in June 1901 and his name appears in the *London Gazette* which was noted by the *Birmingham Mail*.

There isn't a record of what he did on his return but by 1908 he was in trouble. He and Florence now had three children and it appears they were living in the workhouse. He had already been before the courts earlier that year for refusing his allotted task at Erdington Workhouse. It is worth reflecting that just over a hundred years ago in this country someone could face a criminal prosecution for refusing a task at the workhouse. A system that had changed little since the days of *Oliver Twist* where husband and wife and all but very small children were separated on admission was the one that confronted George and his family. Later that year he was caught stealing iron from Bromford Mills. In court Detective Inspector Jackson said he had advised Ravenhill about the bad company he was keeping but that he did not heed the warning. George said that he believed that he was entitled to a pension of £50 a year but he had heard nothing about his claim. The bench said they had tried to help him but he would not help himself and sentenced him to a month in prison.

He was stripped of the VC for this offence and as a result he lost his pension. The fact that six years after the war a man who won an award for outstanding bravery could be treated in this way is an indictment of the punitive attitude to the poor and vulnerable. It was only a year before his death that VCs were reinstated for those convicted of criminal offences. However, worse was to come for the family since in 1911, whilst in the workhouse, with their new baby Alfred just born, Florence and George were persuaded, or more likely compelled, to give up their three children, Lilly, George and Raymond, to the Child Migration scheme. The Custody of Children Act 1891 meant that parents who had to apply for poor relief more than three times lost responsibility for their children. The three children were shipped off to Prince Edward Island on the eastern seaboard of Canada in June of that year.

To understand how Lilly, George and Raymond were sent without their parents with so many other young children to a country far away we need to look at the work of the British Home Children and Child Migrants in Canada. From the late 1860s right up to 1948 over 100,000 children of all ages were emigrated right across Canada to be used at indentured farm labourers and domestics. Believed by Canadians to be orphans, only 2 per cent truly were. These children were sent to Canada by well-known charities including Barnado's and the Salvation Army. The CEO of the Home Children's Advocacy and Research Association said 'Barnado's sent over 30,000 children and was by far the largest organisation sending them.'[5]

For the most part these were not children picked from the streets but came from intact families who through sickness or death of a parent had fallen on hard times. Because there was no social security to help them through these difficult times the family had no alternative to surrender their offspring to these organisations. Families may have moved to find work so if something happened there would no longer be close family able to help with the children and the workhouses were overflowing and provided little solution.

Suffer Little Children

Once in Canada the children were sent to receiving homes right across the country until farmers picked them up or they were sent on to their destinations with a cardboard sign round their necks. There were at least seven applications for every child shipped to Canada.

Emigration was seen as great solution. Younger children were to be fostered, the older ones would help with chores and extended labour would be required of adolescents. Once they were eighteen the indenture would be discharged and living in the fresh air of a Canadian farm was seen as a preferable alternative to a British inner city. However, the truth was often harsh in comparison. The monitoring of children's placements was often neglected and many children found them in worse situations than their old lives. Siblings were separated. Girls assisted not only with housework and children but also worked in the fields. Boy farm workers were often grossly overworked.

Some children were accepted into families as their own and treated as genuine foster children but many suffered. Children could be returned or reassigned and many were moved from one farm to another. Some ran away or simply disappeared; some died from ill health or injuries arising from neglect or abuse. Some took their own way out and committed suicide. Certainly life for many of the children was not happy. At the time the belief in eugenics was strong and so these children were considered inferior stock to their Canadian counterparts and were stigmatised simply because they were poor and needed help. They could be taunted and made to feel shame for being a Home Child. This sense of shame kept some silent about their past even in adult life. However, 10 per cent of Canadians today are descendants of the Home Children.

After their three oldest children left for Canada the next trace of George is when he was living in Oxfordshire. It was from there that he volunteered during the First World War. Serving for three years he was discharged with a disability pension. By the time of his death in 1921 he and Florence had had four more children as well as baby Alfred. They had returned to live in Long Acre in one room in the tenement building in conditions detrimental to their health and they were practically destitute. The funeral was paid for by the Lord Mayor of Birmingham and a grant of £7 10s was made to Florence for clothing for her and the children. John Davison, the Labour MP for Smethwick, raised the case with the Lord Privy Seal in the Commons and asked for help for the widow and children. Lieutenant Colonel the Hon E. F. Stanley in reply said he was aware of the award of the VC but that there were special circumstances which he was communicating with the hon. member. It seems it took George's death to bring any positive response for him and the family. A military funeral was arranged and many people turned out near his home and at Witton Cemetery to pay their respects. However, the family's housing conditions did not improve.

Meanwhile throughout this time George and Florence's children were growing up as Home Children in Canada. The story of their lives there comes to us graphically through a novel written by Louise Ravenhill, George Junior's daughter.[6] It is supplemented by research undertaken by Maureen Noonan.

On arrival in Canada Lilly aged eleven and Raymond aged seven were taken in by a couple called Mr and Mrs Abbot who had sought a boy and girl to foster. They were cared for as the couple's own whereas George junior was picked by a rough farmer called Mr Douglas who needed help on his farm. His story is told as a fiction but Louise Ravenhill has said that she took the story from her father in hours of interviews about his early days on Prince Edward Island. George, aged nine, was taken to Mr Douglas's failing farm where he was not only expected to do the work of an adult but was brutalised at the hands of an angry and embittered man. Louise describes a life that was hard not only for George but also for Mrs Douglas and their increasing brood of children. George worked long hours and was most of the time denied the right to go to school. The inspector for Home Children

Suffer Little Children

on a rare visit to see George's progress took the word of Mr Douglas that the boy was doing well and did not chose to speak to George separately. No doubt in those times this was common practice but it only served to lengthen his time there.

Meanwhile Lilly and Raymond were growing up in a happy home not so far away. In those first two years George was allowed one visit to see his siblings and marvels over the good food and warmth they enjoy. Ashamed to tell anyone of his own miserable existence he returns back to the Douglas household. It is several months more and after a final brutal beating that he runs away to find his siblings and the Abbots again. They realise straightaway what George has been through and when Mr Douglas comes to claim his farm servant back they refuse.

So eventually the three Ravenhill are reunited and brought up by Mr and Mrs Abbot. All were able to complete their education. Lilly, who adopted the full name Lillian, was still in school aged sixteen. She married a William Bumpus who at the age of nineteen had become a petty officer in the Merchant Navy. They were later living in Massachusetts where they had one child. Later, in his twenties George married Mary Edith with whom he had his daughter Louise and three sons. As the novel mimics reality it seems Mary Edith was a young child in the Douglas family who was always kind to George. She had been sent away as an ill child to live with Mrs Douglas's sister in the US and it was many years later that George found her. Raymond Ravenhill returned to Birmingham to find his mother Florence in the 1920s, sadly too late to see his father.

In recent years the Ravenhill family have campaigned to have a fitting memorial to their grandfather and great-grandfather in Victoria Square in Birmingham. One grandson, Kevin, took the VC to Westminster Abbey in 2006. George is commemorated not only by his family but by the British Legion in Chipping Norton where he lived prior to the First World War; they want his name restored to the war memorial there. Kingsbury School in

Tamworth have celebrated his virtues by naming a house after him. It is sad that George himself never saw any of this acclaim. His bravery at Colenso was brushed aside by a society that condemned him for a petty theft committed when he and his family were destitute.

The records of the Lancashire Fusiliers give an insight into the plight of some of their soldiers and relatives. In 1900 Colonel Lees Knowles established a compassionate fund for those suffering or bereaved within the regiment. It was formally constituted at the Minden Dinner given to officers of the 3rd Volunteer Battalion in August 1900 at his home. He made the first contribution by transferring £1,000 to the Trustees of the fund. The Minden Dinner was held annually in commemoration of the regiment's victory at that battle in 1759 where they earned their first battle honours. The records of the fund are interesting in that they give an idea of who was contributing and in what amounts.[7]

They also give clear examples of the kind of problems soldiers and relatives faced. Most were anonymised but two names given within the report enabled research to discover a whole history of the family following the soldiers' deaths. Those concerning John Welsford and Henry Raven are given below.

To give a flavour of the way people were helped these are the records for 1900:

> F.B invalided home from South Africa and unable to follow any employment
> Mrs M.B. widow of T.B. who died in South Africa
> Miss B daughter of an old Crimean veteran in want
> T.C. assisted to go away for his health
> G.D. wounded at Spion Kop, in want
> J.K. suffering from Locomotor ataxy and permanently unable to work
> Mrs L. mother of Sergeant L killed on Spion Kop
> H.P.W. in a very critical state in the R. Workhouse Hospital

W.R. wounded in the spine at Spion Kop and unable to work, his wife is an invalid
E.D.R. wounded at Spion Kop and in want
Mrs R wife of H.R. who, wounded at Spion Kop, died of enteric fever in hospital
Mrs W wife of J.W. killed at Spion Kop
G.W. in hospital
T.W. unable to do anything but light work: wife ill.
J.W. wounded at Spion Kop and temporarily unable to work

Henry Raven was just fourteen when he enlisted with the Lancashire Fusiliers on 14 August 1891. It is likely that he would have joined as a bandboy, either a drummer or bugler who traditionally lead the unit into battle. He had stated on enlistment that he didn't know where he came from. The nearest possible record in the ancestry website indicates a Henry Raven of a similar age who was born in Fermoy, the largest British garrison in Ireland. Before joining he was living with his family in Slade Green, Kent. His father was a labourer aged fifty but it's quite likely that previously he'd been in the military as they were living close to the Woolwich Barracks and that Henry wanted to follow in his father's footsteps.

By 1897 Henry was based at the barracks in Preston and it was here on Christmas Eve that year that he married Catherine Maiddon with their two fathers being the witnesses. Catherine had been born in Aldershot so we can presume that she too was from a military family. In 1898 their daughter Emily was born and the following year Henry set sail for South Africa with his regiment. He was wounded at Spion Kop. It is not clear how badly wounded he was and whether he recovered sufficiently to fight again. What we do know is that by June he was, like so many of his fellow soldiers, ill with enteric and on the 16th of that month he died at a town called Newcastle.

Catherine, left with a one-year-old, sought assistance from the

Transvaal Widows' Fund which was not forthcoming. Just eight days after her young husband's death the entry against her name says simply 'Dismissed'. We know that later in the year she was helped with a grant from the Lancashire Fusiliers' Compassionate Fund but as this was not established until August 1900 there was no question that she had received any money at the time of her husband's death. In 1902 eventually she received a small amount from the soldiers' effects fund. This consisted of any monies owing to the man on death.

By the time of the 1901 census Catherine's mother was living with them and working at home which would have enabled her to look after young Emily while Catherine worked as a wood polisher. Preston was one of the big cotton towns and many of Catherine's female neighbours were listed as cotton weavers and spinners. Catherine did not remarry but in 1907 gave birth to a little boy, called Charles. We have no way of knowing whether her relationship with the father continued but he does not appear in the 1911 census. As the census only records people in the house on that particular night this does not tell us definitively. By this time Catherine's occupation is listed as a charwoman. Emily then twelve and Charles just four are noted as scholars. In the April to June quarter of 1920 Emily, aged twenty-one, married George Sedgewick.

John Welsford from Bideford started his working life as a printer but in June 1889 at the age of 18 he enlisted as a soldier at Camp Wonsford in Devon. It's possible that he worked for a printing works in Exeter that went into liquidation at this time and this prompted his decision to enlist. The 1891 census recorded him as a Gunner in the Royal Artillery serving at a large army encampment near Pembroke in Wales. In 1892, aged twenty-one, he married Charlotte Logan, aged just seventeen and in 1893 they had a little girl, Annie. Happiness was to be short-lived, however, and Charlotte died in 1895. John went back to his home town of Bideford with his young daughter and in 1897 he

Suffer Little Children

married a local girl, Clara Folland. At the time of the 1891 census when she was just fifteen Clara had been one of the servants working for a Joseph Bernard, listed as a Professor of Music in Bideford. After the marriage Clara gave birth to a daughter, Ada, in 1898 and in 1900, a son Richard. When the war came John went to fight in South Africa with the Lancashire Fusiliers. Like so many of his regiment he was caught up in the battles to relieve the Siege of Ladysmith and he was killed on 20 January 1900 at the Battle of Venterspruit. This took place just four days prior to the cataclysmic battle at Spion Kop.

This left Clara a widow, with three children, the last of whom, Richard, was born in January close to the time of John's death in South Africa. The news must have been a terrible blow coming at the time of her son's birth; Richard would never see his father. By the time of the 1901 census Clara was living in Bideford with her stepdaughter, Annie and her young children Ada and Richard. In the same household were Clara's sister, Grace Littlejohns and her young son, Samuel. Grace is listed as a married woman but her husband, a mariner, is presumably away on a voyage. Clara is named as head of the household and is working as a charwoman.

Just eighteen months after John's death in the summer of 1901 Clara remarried. Her new husband, William Welsford, was John's older brother by six years. He is listed in the 1871 census but seems to disappear after that. Records show that from 1890 to 1898 William was in the Navy and fought in the Ashanti campaign in what is present-day Ghana. From this we know that he would have been out of the country for the 1891 census and we can conjecture that if he'd joined aged fourteen in 1881 he would be missing from that year's records too. A connection with the navy is that Clara and he married in Devonport not Bideford; although another is that her sister Grace Littlejohn's family came from there. Devonport was one of the largest naval bases in Britain. In 1902 they had a baby son, also called William, who was born in Bideford. Then in 1903, aged twenty-eight, Clara died leaving not only her baby son but her and John's children, Annie, Ada and Richard. The death certificate shows tragic circumstances; Clara died of Heart Disease, Childbirth, Haemorrhage and Exhaustion. Her husband William was present at the death. In the days before a properly-funded health service and where maternity knowledge was poor such deaths were not uncommon. Clara would have died not knowing what the future of her children would be.

It is on record that Clara had received a grant from the Lancashire Fusiliers' Compassionate fund of £3. SSAFA's records which were anonymised show that a widow in Bideford with three children who may to have been Clara received some support at the time. This would have been in the form of a grant; not an ongoing weekly payment. Clara was recommended for the grant from the Compassionate Fund by a Miss Mary Molesworth, a lady of independent means from Bideford who had said that Clara was 'particularly deserving'. Miss Molesworth's father had been a magistrate in Bideford but her mother Sarah was originally from Littleborough in Lancashire and Mary was visiting that area at the time of the 1901 census. A link with the Lancashire regiments is likely. This pattern of charity is very much in the mould of the 'lady bountiful'. It is fortunate that such kindnesses were available as the country had sent so many men out to fight with no provision for their dependents in its aftermath. Certainly she received nothing from the Transvaal Widows' Fund; the record there says baldly Clara Welsford 'Remarried now dead'. We can only speculate on motives long gone but the fact that so many widows of the conflict remarried so quickly implies their fear of being left without support. In Clara's case this would have been preferable to being a charwoman or having no support for her children.

After her death the circumstances for her children become hazy. We do know that their stepfather who was also their uncle

Suffer Little Children

William remarried in 1905 to a widow with two children of her own. By the 1911 census he was living with her, her children and his own son William in Bideford and was working as a labourer. Annie, John's oldest daughter was a young adult by then, and was living with an aunt in Bideford and working as collar maker. Ada and Richard seemed to have disappeared off the face of the earth and yet were not to be found in death registers either. Different variations on their names yielded no results until the emigration records were checked. Ada aged ten and Richard just eight had been sent on the Child Migration scheme to Canada. On 21 May 1908 they sailed with many other children organised by Barnado's from the port of Liverpool to Quebec in Canada. Just like the Ravenhill children they were part of the massive child migration scheme to Canada.

We do not know what happened to these very young children when their mother died in 1903. Did they stay with the stepfather or not, and did this change in 1905 when he remarried? Clara's sister Grace had shared a house with her and the children in 1901 but where was Grace after Clara's death? Placing the children in a home and allowing them to be sent abroad may have been the result of financial constraints. Nowadays Child Benefit and the Guardians' allowance might have eased the burden for either set of relatives. Were they convinced by the authorities that life in the fresh air of Canada would be good for the children? Emigration because of the difficulties of farming had been a common feature of Devon throughout the nineteenth century and even smaller ports like Bideford had seen off boatloads of emigrants to Canada and North America. Perhaps that normalised the decisions of those family members who agreed to Ada and Richard going. There is no record of where the children were living in the interim. The North Devon Archives do not have records of children's admissions to orphanages or workhouses at this time and Barnardo's who may have cared for them in this period only allow access to their archives for proven relatives. However, the fact that these children who lost their father in the war and their mother not long after were sent abroad to such an uncertain future is an indictment not only on childcare policies at the time but also how the families of servicemen were treated.

It appears though that the Welsford children's story had a twist and happily a positive one. On arrival in Canada Ada was recorded on the Hazelbrae memorial for girls lodged at that home while Richard may have been sent to the 'distribution' centre for boys in Toronto. However, sometime before the 1911 census was taken they had been reunited under the care of a Dr and Mrs Gilchrist in Simcoe, East Ontario .The couple appear to have been in their forties with no existing children. Records suggest that Ada and Richard were the lucky ones of the Home Children by being adopted in this way and that they were able to complete their schooling. Richard must have gone to college since when he married in 1927 his profession was given as 'druggist' which may be chemist. Ada, as would have been the norm for middle-class ladies then, was a housewife. Her husband, Luke Pearsall, was an educated and successful man who in the 1950s on a visit to London was, with his wife, a guest at the Canadian Embassy. The couple took a first-class berth on the voyage which for Ada would have been a very far cry from the steerage passage she had shared going to Canada with other Barnado's children in 1908.

Chapter 10

THEY SERVED AND MANY SERVED AGAIN

It was a mere twelve years and two months from the end of the Boer War to the outbreak of the First World War. Men who had fought in South Africa went on to fight or serve in some capacity in this next war.

Whilst researching this book many people kindly provided information about their relatives including photos of medals and men in uniform. They did not always have the full details of where they served in the war but were clearly proud of their participation there and sometimes in the Great War which followed. Some men's stories during the war have been told in earlier chapters and here their stories are concluded. Others are new.

Andrew Ernest Smith was of German descent. His father, Ernst Schmidt, a Prussian soldier, had arrived in England in the late 1850s and Andrew was born in Stroud, Gloucestershire, in 1869. On his marriage certificate from 1894 it stated that he was a 'valet presser' to a senior officer and therefore likely served in the Grenadier Guards. His grandson, Gordon Smith, did not know a great deal about his role in South Africa but he did receive the Queen's and King's Medal for service there. In the 1901 census his wife stated that he was away fighting in South Africa. They had seven children in all and one son, having lied about his age, was killed in the First World War. Andrew dyed his hair black and re-enlisted, **lying** about his age saying he was thirty-two when he was actually forty-seven! His intent was to 'avenge' the death of his son, which his grandson explained that this was something a number of men did at the time. Andrew was a drinker, a problem perhaps exacerbated by his wartime experiences and died at the age of fifty-four in 1924.

John Meardon was from Hatherleigh in rural mid-Devon. He had left school at the age of nine to work on a local farm where he was in charge of the horses. As a youngster he enlisted in the Royal Engineers and saw service in the Punjab before going to South Africa where he was involved in all of the fierce fighting for the relief of Ladysmith. He spent thirty-three years in the army rising finally to the rank of Sergeant-Major. Returning home to Hatherleigh, he worked as the local postman and was keen on growing flowers. His well-deserved peaceful existence there must have seemed in stark contrast to what he had experienced in the battlefield.

Harry Churchill Beet was born in Bingham, Nottinghamshire in 1875, one of five children. His father, a stonemason, died in an accident at work in February 1892 and shortly afterwards Harry enlisted saying he was eighteen years old. He served in India and then he and his brother, William Churchill Beet, both served in South Africa with the Mounted Infantry of the Derbyshire Regiment. Harry was awarded the Victoria Cross for his bravery at Wakkerstroom (in the Transvaal) where he guarded an injured comrade from the Imperial Yeomanry. Harry bound up his wounds and kept watch over him all afternoon, keeping the Boers at bay by firing at them. He was himself under heavy fire throughout that time. He received the VC from the Duke of York (later George V) at Natal in August 1901. On return home he remained in the army until 1904 and thereafter stayed in the reserves for another year.

In 1906 he and his family emigrated to Canada where, at the outbreak of the First World War, he enlisted in the Saskatchewan Light Horse. He then transferred to the Canadian Army where he was commissioned in January 1916 as a Lieutenant. In January

They Served and Many Served Again

1918 he retired from the army with the honorary rank of Captain aged forty-three. But his military career did not end there and when war broke out again in 1939 he joined the Canadian 110th Infantry Reserve Company, a veteran guard unit. Discharged because of his age in 1942 he went on to join the Royal Canadian Mounted Police and spent the rest of the war guarding Japanese prisoners of war. When he died in 1946 he was buried with full military honours. His medals are in the regimental museum in Nottingham Castle.

Samuel Young, from the small Dorset village of Semley, volunteered for the county's Yeomanry in late 1899 at the age of nineteen years. He was in action many times receiving bars for battles at Belfast, Diamond Hill, Johannesburg, Orange Free State and Cape Colony. He received the Queen's Pipe on behalf of his unit and was chosen to represent the Dorset Yeomanry at the occasion of Edward VII's coronation. According to the local paper, upon his arrival back in Dorset he was

> ... given a hearty reception and it was said he would have been more feted if his modesty had not prevented him from letting the village know of his arrival. Nevertheless his fellow villagers took the horses from the carriage and insisted on pulling home the popular hero, whose successful career and achievements they had watched with much keen interest during the two and a half years' absence from the place of his birth ... Although he has been on the move constantly in South Africa, has fought in many of the battles, had one or two horses shot from under him and has had many lucky escapes, he has been fortunate enough to arrive home without a wound of any description.

His last action was at Rooival on 11 April 1902 and he, like others left at the end of the war had been involved in 'making drives', which meant driving the Boer commandos into the blockhouse lines. After the war he went into farming and, although he volunteered for service in 1914, he was exempted because of the contribution his farm made to the community.

Trooper Burbridge from Wyke Regis also fought with the Dorset Yeomanry. He was wounded in the hand and invalided home. As with Samuel Young, he had an uproarious welcome from the people of his village and again it involved taking the horses out of the carriage and pulling him by sheer strength up to the village square. Everyone wanted to shake his hand and the parish councillor gave him his blessing saying he never had the privilege of welcoming home a war hero. Later he took up work as a coal merchant, married and had children.

In the previous chapter **Alfred Whitby** was writing to his mother on Boxing Day 1901 to reassure her that he was not hurt in the Battle of Groenkop. Since he was stationed at Elands River, between Bethlehem and Harrismith, it is likely that he was involved in building the blockhouse lines or driving the Boers towards these lines. After the war he returned to London safe and sound with the expectation that he would return to his previous employment as an invoice clerk at a gasworks in High Holborn. However, as they could not offer him a position they provided him with a glowing reference. One wonders how many volunteers for the war found themselves in this position. Alfred did obtain work as a foreman at Hayes Wharf in the London docks where his job was to pick men on a daily basis for casual work. His daughter commented that he was an intelligent man and the work needed to be sensitively handled since it concerned men's livelihoods and sometimes fights broke out. It is known that at home he had a trunk with his Boer War uniform in it, but his family said that he never talked of the war. Before he went he was a pleasant, outgoing young man but afterwards he could be morose, did not like loud noises which included children playing and he wouldn't participate in his wife's weekly dancing trips. We do not know exactly what he saw but it's quite possible given his location that he would have been involved in drives against the Boers and maybe guarding a concentration camp (there was one nearby at Harrismith). He died aged fifty-three of a sudden case of viral pneumonia. His nineteen-year-old daughter was distressed because she felt she had never really known her father. We can never really know why Alfred had such a change of personality but bearing the burden of what he experienced and what he may have been ordered to do is likely to have pressed hard on him.

Men from all over Britain, Ireland and the Empire fought in this war. We have already seen how many men from Dundee fought out in South Africa but some came from even further north. **Donald Meilklejohn** from Castletown in Caithness was twenty when he enlisted in the Scottish Horse Regiment. His granddaughter Elizabeth remembers seeing his spurs as a child. He would have had training at Aldershot before leaving for South Africa after enlisting as a trooper on 31 January 1901. By the following year he was described as an engineer (marine) and was discharged on 3 September 1902. As with many of the men who served in South Africa he continued in military service working as a marine engineer for the Admiralty in the First World War. By the Second World War he was a civilian engineer at Fort George Military Base in Morayshire where he died in 1944. Records are held at the Dunkeld archives.

Jesse Hall was from Staffordshire and joined the Queens Royal Rifles. He was wounded by shrapnel at Spion Kop. His grandson has a childhood memory of Jesse talking about the people in South Africa. He had shown a great respect for the Zulus and Boers as fighters but regarded the other black people as 'fuzzey wuzzies'. We have already seen that such attitudes were endemic amongst British troops brought up with notions of racism and imperialism. Despite earlier injuries Jesse fought in the First World War until discharged as being unfit in 1916.

George Taylor was a regular soldier who had volunteered

before the war. Walking from Somerset where he was born, he was first refused enlistment by the Worcestershire Regiment but, determined to join up, he carried on walking until he was taken on by the Queen's Royal Rifles. During the war he was shot in the foot and when he was an older man this was confirmed by a chiropodist. After the war he went to work at Thomas Piggots in Smethwick as an engineer. Once retired in the early 1960s he went to live with first one of his sons and then another. His grandson Adrian, aged about seven at that time, described him as a rather ill-tempered man and not particularly well-disposed to his grandchildren. However, Adrian is proud of his grandfather's record in the war.

William Wilcock was one of the many Cornishmen who went to fight in South Africa. Born in Camborne in 1867 he moved to Penzance aged fourteen to work on the railways. Part of his duties was to transport fish from the port across the country. In 1891 his train was snowed-in near Redruth for four days without food. Two hundred men came to rescue him although unfortunately a guard was killed in an accident with the engine that arrived to pull him out. His service in the Boer War earned him the Freedom of Penzance and a silver casket as a gift. He was clearly well thought of since not only was he picked to attend Edward VII's coronation but he was also to be a bodyguard to Sir Alfred Milner, the British High Commissioner. Edward VII was previously the Duke of Cornwall and had a long association with the local regiment. Following the war he worked as a fireman and was mentioned several times in *The Cornishman* for bravery in entering smoke-filled rooms to rescue people. William lived to the age of eighty-eight and his funeral in his home town was attended by the Mayor and many other dignitaries.

War can have unexpected consequences. **William and Charles Gill** were brothers from the small village of Avonwick in Devon. Their father had died of phthitis, a form of tuberculosis, aged just twenty-four. William was just two years old and Charles was born

They Served and Many Served Again

posthumously. Their mother subsequently married Francis Baskwill and four more children followed. As a young man William enlisted in the Royal Engineers and had served in Malta and Gibraltar before going to South Africa. Charles joined the 18th Hussars. He was wounded first at Wagon Hill on 6 January 1900, the battle in which **Charles Webber** lost a leg and **James Boseley** had both his leg and arm amputated. We do not know the extent of Charles Gill's injuries but he continued to serve and was killed in a skirmish at Roodeport near Johannesburg on 2 February 1901. Lance Corporal Gill is recorded with some of the 400 other Devon men on the memorials in Exeter Cathedral. Before the war Charles had been engaged to a local girl called Carrie Moore. When he did not return home she married his brother, William! Barbara, William's granddaughter, did not know the story behind this. Perhaps there had been a pre-existing affection or maybe this was simply a practical solution. By all accounts they had a good life together running the local post office with William also acting as postman, barber and shoemaker.

The war would have unforeseen consequences in other ways. **William Neilson Duncan**, a tram conductor from Dundee, worked in South Africa on the railways, an occupation that a number of British emigrants seemed to follow. During the Boer War he joined Kitchener's fighting scouts and in 1902 he joined the Scottish Horse. His grandson, Mac, has put a lot of effort into tracing him but sadly he never found out what happened and why he stayed on in South Africa. After leaving Dundee William seemed to be sending money home and looking after his family. Mac has sent me photos of his father at school, better dressed than most of the other kids and wearing shoes. A photo showed a family who were doing reasonably well. His father also had his school lunch with the teachers eating potato soup and decent bread. Eventually after the grandmother refused to go and join him in South Africa the money dried up. Like so many women in Dundee his grandmother had been a mill worker.

Charles Henry Messenger was from Worcestershire but served with the Devonshire Regiment. Born in 1869, he first served in Burma and later in South Africa. He would have seen fierce fighting in the early part of the war gaining bars for Laings Nek, the Transvaal, the relief of Ladysmith, Tugela Heights and the Orange Free State. He also served in the First World War even though at the age of forty-five he was technically too old. This echoes the story of Andrew Smith and it is likely that late in the war the army was happy to turn a blind eye to this as they became desperate for recruits.

The diary of **W. H. Francis** provides a good account of his trials and adventures during the war. After his final skirmish with the Boers, when he was seriously injured, he was eventually brought home on 8 March 1901 but not before contracting another serious stomach complaint and having both eyes bitten by mosquitoes. The diary records that many of his comrades died on the return journey. At home he was eventually able to carry on with his work as a newsagent. He, too, volunteered for the First World War and, with the Royal Fusiliers, served in German East Africa where, following injuries, he was again invalided home. The extent of his injuries meant he could not work again but he busied himself with many charitable and voluntary activities including the British Legion, the local Conservative Association and sat on the War Pensions Committee which would seem fitting work for him. His injuries undoubtedly shortened his life and he died aged just fifty-three.

Herbert John Browning came from Liskeard in east Cornwall, which was the same area as Emily Hobhouse. Indeed it was there that she and Lloyd George spoke out against the war and an angry crowd had shouted them down. Herbert Browning was educated at Liskeard Grammar School. He went to South Africa as a telegraph operator in 1896. Based in Port Elizabeth in the south-east of the country he travelled around to fulfil his duties. He joined the South African Rifles and fought for the

British in the Boer War and subsequently in the First World War having joined up in October 1915. He served in both German and Portuguese East Africa where he died at Murembe in May 1918 having contracted blackwater fever whilst on service.

John Ball was another Cornishman who went to fight in the war. Originally in the Territorial Army he was sent to South Africa in 1900 aged just twenty. In his case war did, at least, provide an unexpected gift. Prior to his departure he had become engaged to Elizabeth (Bessie) whom he had met at Rosenannon Methodist Church. Like many young women Bessie worked as a housekeeper and must have seen her young man go with some trepidation. While he was away John bought a piece of local gold in Bloemfontein which he had made into a ring for Bessie on his return.

On his return home they married, farmed at Tom's Tenement, near St Breock and raised twelve children. They remained tenants of the Duchy of Cornwall for the duration of their working life on the farm. Two of their children still survive and it is the wife of Steve Ball who provided the story, remarking: 'How hard it must have been for a young farm boy to be caught up in such a volatile situation in a distant land. I like to think that the gold ring that John carried with him would have given him hope for the future. It is a ring with a very special meaning, one which remains in the family more than a 100 years later.' It is a lovely story and one where at least one soldier brought home some of the gold over which the war was fought.

We have already seen that doctors who volunteered from Britain played a major part in the war. **Dr. William Ashford** departed for South Africa in April 1900. He was then an assistant house surgeon and a member of the Royal College of Surgeons, having trained at St Thomas's in London where he was also a successful rugby player. Whilst there he met his future wife, Elise Irwin, who was a Red Cross nurse. Upon their return they married and settled happily in Dr Ashford's home town of Topsham near

Exeter. There he established a medical practice at their house in Riversmeet Terrace. At the commencement of the First World War he and Elise ran a Voluntary Aid Detachment (VAD) hospital from the house. Dr Ashford was a keen photographer and took a variety of interesting photos whilst out in South Africa.

Robert Slattery was the young man who had such a difficult childhood in Liverpool following the death of his mother. He served in and around Kimberley. Thankfully Robert survived and returned to Lancashire. His first job was at Burnley Workhouse where, over time, he rose to become officer in charge of the male block. We also have records of Thomas Stone's brother-in-law working at Blackburn workhouse at that time. From 1907 he worked on the newly-introduced trams in the town. Together with his wife Elizabeth (Pickup) he joined the St John's Ambulance brigade and he was a member of the League of Frontiersmen, rising to Sergeant-Major. He and his wife learned Esperanto and letters to each other show their language skills.

In 1914 he joined up and as part of the RAMC went to the military hospital at Netley. He served out in Egypt and was recommended four times for the Distinguished Conduct Medal. He was demobbed in 1918 and probably as a result of his service abroad he died in 1921 from the effects of malaria. This was acknowledged at his funeral when it was said: 'He died as truly in the service of his country as if on the battlefield.' He was just forty-six years old.

In Chapter 2 it was noted that **Albert Skedgell**, at seventeen, was the youngest sailor to be landed with the gun from HMS *Doris*. When the ship returned in May 1901 the people of Plymouth and Devonport gave them a rapturous welcome which would have been mixed with sadness as well since they had lost comrades in the fighting. Their names are displayed to this day on the side of the gun which serves as a memorial in Devonport Park. Despite the importance of Plymouth and Devonport in naval history these sailors are the only people in the city memorialised for serving in the Boer War. The Boer War memorial on Plymouth Hoe, whilst recording the battles, is dedicated to just one man, Queen Victoria's grandson Prince Christian Victor of Schleswig-Holstein, who died of enteric in Pretoria. After being away for four years in total Albert was granted just two weeks leave which he spent visiting his family and old friends. His life in the navy continued with long periods of time at sea but with some assignments at home. In April 1907 he married Alice Reeves, a local girl who he had first met when she was twelve years old whilst working as a delivery boy. Life in the navy meant that Albert would be away at sea a great deal. After a short lived honeymoon he was off for five months. Despite this, the couple had a happy married life and as their family expanded they lived in a variety of rented cottages in the Kingsbridge area. In all Albert and Alice raised six children.

Albert was still in the navy when the First World War broke out. He fought in both the Dardanelles and later at the Battle of Jutland. Unscathed throughout the Boer War, it was in this battle that his ship, HMS *Marlborough*, was hit by a torpedo and Albert was wounded. He managed to stay with his gun and continued firing but ultimately was confined to the sickbay and placed in the Royal Naval Hospital in Plymouth on his return home. The wounds were bad enough to mean he was medically discharged from the navy and would need to walk with a stick. His naval pension ensured the family were better off than many agricultural labourers. He was a mechanically-minded man and was soon able to earn a living mending threshing machines in the area. However, with a growing family the vegetable patch behind their cottage and trips out rabbiting were a great help in feeding everyone.

By the Second World War Albert was an active member of the Civil Defence in Totnes where the family were currently living. Tom, one of his sons, was unlucky enough to be captured by the Japanese and spent four years in a prisoner-of-war camp, an experience that left him with recurring nightmares for many years. Albert's life was dogged by different wars but the comradeship of his fellow sailors and, more importantly, a happy marriage gave him a contentment in life. He died in September 1950 aged sixty-eight. Clearly a much-loved family man, his grandson, Roy Tucker, has written a small book which reflects his life and that of working country people in the first half of the twentieth century.

Mr Curnow was the stretcher-bearer who carried out his duties during the early, fierce battles of Colenso and Spion Kop. His diary provides a unique insight into the life of medics who also witnessed horrific and often gruesome scenes which must have remained with him and others for a long time afterwards. Mr Curnow returned to Plymouth after the war, married and had two daughters and a son. He always worked in the dockyard. A religious man, he was known to read the Bible every day. Perhaps his experiences in South Africa heightened the need for his faith. The diary was passed to Mr Booth whose family shared the house off North Hill, Plymouth and who commented that he was a gentleman, being kind to them when their own father died.

Charles Henry Ruddock was one of the 'Ragged Hundred' (mentioned in his funeral oration) who ate contaminated barley during the Siege of Ladysmith. Some of his comrades died as a result of this. Fortunately for Charles, he returned home safely where he worked variously as a prison warder and a clerk in the labour exchange where, his granddaughter reported, he maintained a tough attitude towards the claimants. Clearly a man with an ongoing love for the military, he used to attend military reunions wearing his red uniform coat. He died in 1950 and in common with many of the Boer War veterans at this time he received a full military funeral.

As noted earlier, **Arthur Wilson** provided a description of the siege of Kimberley and his account of life as a boy soldier. He was a career soldier and remained with the army in South Africa until 1908 when day-to-day governance was handed over to the Boers.

He returned to England and was based at Tidworth Camp in York. By 1913 he had been promoted to Regimental Sergeant-Major. He describes how he was playing tennis on 4 August 1914 when a telegraph boy brought to him the order to mobilise. His regiment left for France within ten days and he was engaged in ongoing fighting during the Great War. He retired in 1919 having achieved the permanent rank of Captain in the Scots Greys, the regiment he had joined twenty years earlier. His grandson proudly maintains his extensive diary, which he wrote whilst nearing his end in 1944, and also retains a number of artefacts from the Boer War.

Fred Griffin was the young man from Honiton, Devon, who had worked as a private security guard in Kimberley's diamond mines. He wrote graphically about the siege that took place there. He had been optimistic about the prospects for South Africa telling his mother that it was the up-and-coming country for emigration. After the war Fred continued working for the police until 1908 when he was made redundant following a reorganisation. Following this he undertook a career in gold mining having obtained a certificate in blasting from the Inspector of Mines in Pretoria. So in his late thirties he had little choice but to embark on a career which would have been injurious to his health.

In 1915 he married Kate Julia Berry Paterson and they moved to Springs, a coal- and goldmining town seventy-five miles from Johannesburg. He married later in life which is surprising as Fred showed himself in his diary to be a young man with a genuine sympathy for women and other people in distress. However, his work may have left him isolated. Sadly their marriage ended after only three years when Kate died in August 1918. Fred lived another eleven years. On his death certificate he was listed as an underground gold miner and the cause of death was given as pulmonary silicosis and tuberculosis. Presumably the two were connected. There were no offspring from his marriage to Kate and he left all of his estate, £99 6 shillings and 3 pence to his mother back home in Devon.

William Coldridge was one of eight children born in Exeter in 1868. When he went to South Africa to fight as part of the Bedford Yeomanry he would have been thirty-two years old. He fought under General Buller at Ladysmith, Rietfontein and Lydenburg and received the Distinguished Conduct Medal at Elandslaagte. Interestingly his great nephew, Phil Densham, tells the story that William was offered but declined a commission preferring to remain a warrant officer. Apparently he did this in view of the expense involved in being an officer. This reflects once again the chasm between the officer class and the ranks which has been commented on previously. It has already been noted how the officers expected their lives to be cushioned in the theatre of war whether through receiving better rations or taking manservants on campaign with them. William married Hilda Woolford and they had a daughter, Eileen. He fought again in the First World War and, aged nearly fifty, died in Flanders on 21 July 1918. It is surmised that he died of the influenza that was beginning to sweep through the troops at this time.

Thomas Randell was almost thirty when he went off to the Boer War. He had already served in the Royal Artillery since 1889 when he had joined up as a nineteen-year-old, serving in India throughout this period. He had been placed in the reserves the year prior to the Boer War and then fought there for the duration of the war. His discharge papers state that he wished to be employed in ironworking and indeed he became a tube drawer. In the First World War he served in the recruitment office in Birmingham Town Hall. He and his wife ran a shop in Aston and a younger relative had a memory of him playing Patience upstairs while his wife served in the shop.

Frederick Hands was a sailor operating out of Plymouth, whilst his mother and sisters lived in east London. He had trained as a farrier in the 1890s. He married Henrietta in 1900 but not long after was bound for South Africa. Together with his comrades on HMS *Blanche* he landed at Lamberts Bay in the Western Cape early in 1901. There is an account of the ship's journey by a colleague, Charles Lewis, who kept a diary. We know many horses were sent and many were lost in battle but Charles Lewis describes how they brought them ashore with the sailors holding the halters and swimming with them. The Staffordshire Regiment disembarked through thick fog but when it cleared they could see that the rocks were covered in 'puffins' (*sic* – this may refer to penguins that do breed in this vicinity)! One of the Staffordshire soldiers called them 'doods', in a strong regional accent, which made them all laugh. All of this would have been witnessed by Frederick as well who received the Queen's South Africa medal with a clasp for the Cape Colony. He remained with the navy during the First World War and saw action in Belgium in 1914 at the defence of Antwerp. A year later he was in the Dardanelles and was noted for valuable service at Gallipoli, where he was injured and invalided out when shrapnel lodged in his finger. Frederick died aged sixty-four in 1938 from a cerebral thrombosis. He was still living in Plymouth.

Morris Johnstone served in the Black Watch and hailed, like so many of his comrades, from Dundee. Shortly after the terrible battle at Magersfontein which had claimed so many men from the Regiment he was based at a lookout post near Thabanchu in the Orange Free State. High on a kopje they could communicate with other lookout posts by heliograph or by signal lamps when it grew too dark. Morris wrote home about New Year's Eve 1900, since it was an historic one marking not just a New Year but a new century, being spent so far from home. It is interesting to see the contrast in food supplies. Some troops on the march having nothing but bully beef and dry biscuits but fortunately they were provided with very good eatables. These included turkeys, geese, mutton pie, plum pudding and cake. Afterwards they smoked their pipes and chatted about friends back home and wished themselves a speedy return to Bonnie Scotland. At midnight Auld Lang Syne was sung and they continued through the night singing Scottish and other melodies. It would have made an evocative scene seeing these men wearing their kilts on a small African hilltop so far from their homeland. Morris returned home safely at the end of the war, moving in 1907 to run the post office in Paisley near Glasgow. As with many others he also served in the First World War with the Black Watch. He had retired by 1942 and during the Second World War he was a platoon sergeant with the Home Guard and credited with being a crack shot.

Whilst researching this book I often wondered if any of my own ancestors had any involvement with the Boer War. My English grandparents would have been nine and ten years old at the outbreak of the war. Both lived in London with my grandmother, Rhoda Robinson (nee Wolf) living in the centre near Warren Street at the time of the 1901 census. My grandfather, George Robinson, lived in Leyton. Had they been taken to see the soldiers marching off or even witnessed the euphoric celebrations following the Relief of Mafeking? Quite recently, after reviewing certain family papers, I discovered the birth and marriage certificate of Daisy Reeve, née Robinson, one of my great-aunts. Through the Ancestry website I was able to explore the 1901 census and there I found another great-aunt, Alice Mary, aged twenty-two, who had been married with a one-year-old daughter, also named Alice. However, her husband, **Robert Milburn**, was absent and it occurred to me that he might have been away from the family home serving with the army in South Africa. Searching for his name on their website revealed a link to a family tree which explained that he had emigrated to Canada. In addition a distant relative had uploaded other information including photographs and newspaper cuttings, one of which was a report of Robert's funeral which stated that he had been a veteran of the Boer War! My great-uncle, Robert, served with the Coldstream Guards throughout the war. Records show that he gained medal clasps for Belmont, Modder River, Driefontein, Johannesburg, Diamond Hill and Belfast and received both the Queen's and King's South Africa Medals. He was thus engaged in fighting across a wide geographical area and involved in many difficult engagements and yet it seems he was fortunate to have escaped injury.

Robert was from farming stock in Nottinghamshire. Sadly his father was gored to death by a bull and following this tragedy his mother took the children back to live with her parents. Robert was born around 1871 and there is a photo taken in Clapham, London, which shows him in his uniform. This indicates that he enlisted in 1888. He was discharged in 1894 at the age of twenty-two years and eight months. He was 5ft 8½in tall with blue eyes, brown hair and a fresh complexion and considered of very good conduct. Presumably he stayed in the reserves since he was called up for the war in 1899. He and Alice had married in May of that year. By the 1911 census the family were living and farming back in Nottinghamshire and had another child, a son. It appears that they took advantage of one of the many emigration schemes and set sail for Canada. Living first at Burlington, then Moulton Township, they lived and worked as farmers. Robert died in April 1933 but his wife, Alice outlived him until 1961.

AFTERWORD

This book is subtitled *Soldiers of a Forgotten War*. The Boer War, which finished just twelve years before the Great War, was undoubtedly eclipsed by that monumental world war. It was forgotten, however, not simply because it preceded such large-scale carnage embroiling nations from around the globe. The act of 'forgetting' was convenient too. When the tactics employed by the British high command, after their capture of Pretoria in June 1900, became known there was a palpable shock in other countries. The farm burnings and the deaths in the concentration camps stained the reputation of the British Empire. Many in Britain as well condemned the strategy that Lord Kitchener had promulgated and the government that supported it. Nevertheless, those who did challenge and criticise the actions of the British Army were still known pejoratively as Pro-Boers and many disputed the truth of the horrific reports as they emerged from South Africa. Emily Hobhouse, who exposed the terrible treatment of women and children in the concentration camps, was ostracised back home in Britain. And yet she was feted in South Africa for exposing those appalling conditions and has remained a national heroine there. She is the only non-South African to have had her ashes interred in the National Women's Monument in Bloemfontein alongside former President Steyn and his wife. Today, in the United Kingdom, she is hardly known outside her native Cornwall. It was the ordinary British soldier who was commanded to implement these policies and, we can see in the testimony of Joseph Collet, the revulsion felt by some of those who were ordered to drag women and children from their homes and witness the destruction of their farms and livelihoods. For many it was a memory that they buried deeply

Afterword

and it may be that they were instructed not to discuss it on their return home.

It seems unfair that all those who participated, either as regular soldiers or as volunteers, have been all but forgotten and the problems their families experienced lost in the mist of time. The various regimental records of those who died usually provide one line to the ranks of the privates and able seaman. The officers, by contrast, are remembered through the provision of a mini-biography which includes their public school, whose class they were in and their army ranks. One of the objectives of this book was to uncover the stories of those ordinary soldiers and their families. The fact that there are no living survivors provided a considerable challenge. The testimonies uncovered from relatives and through the soldiers' letters remaining in archives have helped illuminate these men's lives and have greatly helped to provide an understanding of this war and its aftermath from the perspective of the ordinary soldier and their family.

In writing this book it would not have been possible to provide, from afar, a glimpse into the experiences of these ordinary soldiers and their families without those people who came forward to tell me about their grandparents and great grandparents who were most generous with their stories, photos and letters. I am eternally grateful to them.

LOOKING FOR YOUR BOER WAR ANCESTOR

When I embarked on this research I wondered how many direct stories I could find from soldiers in that war. All of those who fought and their parents and partners who were bereaved had all passed away by the 1950s or 1960s. Whilst some had their service in the war mentioned in their funeral orations this conflict seemed to have fairly minor significance against the two world wars that followed. In 1999 the 100th anniversary of its beginning in the countryside of Natal it received scant attention in the UK.

Initially I had discovered some diaries and letters in archives and museums around the country – see below – but I wasn't until I 'went public' that personal accounts and mementoes came alive. In the summer of 2014 I wrote to newspapers across the country asking their readers to send in any stories or mementoes of their Boer War ancestors. Requests went to newspapers from the west of Cornwall to the north of Scotland. Not every newspaper followed up my request but from those that did I received replies from Dundee, John O'Groats, Lancashire, Staffordshire, Swansea, Brighton, Dorset, Devon and Cornwall. I had written to the Devon History Society which yielded many replies including one from relatives now in Canada. My own local paper, the *Plymouth Evening Herald*, gave me a double-paged spread which I was very grateful for. None of these people's stories had ever gone into museums or archives but the eagerness to make contact showed their pride in these long forgotten memories. Most of the people who contacted me were the grandchildren of the soldiers; one or two of them remembered their relatives when they were children. Others had been told about these relatives. What was clear was there was a danger if the memories were not recorded now they would simply be lost.

Looking For Your Boer War Ancestor

The people thus contacted had some sense of their relative and their role in a war long ago but not everyone researching this would know whether their grandfather, great grandfather or great uncle fought there. For many nowadays the popularity of family history means people have delved into their family backgrounds. The following websites are invaluable in researching this.

The Roll of Honour – Lest we Forget www.boer-war.com is an invaluable source of information including list of battles, location of memorials, comprehensive list of regiments and a searchable database for individual soldiers. The site is free to use but welcomes donations as it is compiled entirely by volunteers.

I have taken the following list of regiments from their website:

Argyll and Sutherland Highlanders
Bedford Regiment
The Black Watch (Royal Highlanders)
Cameronians (Scottish Rifles)
Durham Light Infantry
Gloucester Regiment
Gordon Highlanders
Hampshire Regiment
Highland Light Infantry
Imperial Yeomanry Battalions
Imperial Yeomanry Companies
King's (Liverpool) Regiment
King's Royal Rifle Corps
King's Shropshire Light Infantry
Lancashire Fusiliers
Lincolnshire Regiment
Loyal North Lancashire Regiment
Norfolk Regiment
Northumberland Fusiliers

Oxfordshire Light Infantry
Royal Army Medical Corps (RAMC)
Royal Dublin Fusiliers
Royal Engineers
Royal Garrison Artillery (RGA)
Royal Scots (Lothian Regiment)
Royal Scots Greys (2nd Dragoons)
Royal Warwickshire Regiment
Seaforth Highlanders
Somerset Light Infantry
South Lancashire Regiment (Prince of Wales Volunteers)
South Staffordshire Regiment
Suffolk Regiment
Worcestershire Regiment
Yorkshire Regiment
Royal Navy and Training Ships

Find my Past – this website has a searchable database where you can look for a soldier ancestor. Of course knowing details such as his place and date of birth and the regiment in which he served will help.

Ancestry.co.uk. has many sites which will help you to track down your ancestor. It has a list of casualties of the war; census, marriage, births, baptism, christenings, deaths and burials. In this way you can trace related members of the family. Recently added is a database of soldiers' effects – this details to whom possessions and monies went on the soldiers' death. Often the mother was given as the next of kin indicating how young some of the soldiers were. As we saw in Chapter 6, if the boys were from an orphanage the effects were given back to the home. You can also access emigration records on this site. This would enable you to see if your ancestor emigrated after the war or indeed as we found that orphaned children were sent abroad on child

Looking For Your Boer War Ancestor

migration schemes. See below for details of British Home Children in Canada.

Forces Records – hold a database of soldiers' names for wars back to Victorian times. This site is useful particularly if you don't know the regiment.

These three websites allow a search for individual soldiers and the battles they were involved in. They are accessible by subscription. Some can be accessed through a local library card.

A2A stands for Access to Archives and is the Database of the National Archives. It is an invaluable resource and gives access to archives across the country through a simple search facility. Entering such terms as 'Boer war soldier', 'Boer War soldiers' families' will bring up references both to records at the National Archives and regionally based archives. The National Archives, is based at Kew in West London,

> Address:
> Richmond Road,
> Twickenham,
> Surrey.
> 0208 876 3444

It is open to the public Tuesday to Saturday. You will be asked to register for a reader's card before using the archives.

The Archives hold the records of many soldiers who fought in the Boer War:

- Regular Army Soldiers are in WO 97.
- Later Pension claims can be found in WO 148 (between 1901 and 1904) and PMG 9/48-50 for later claims.
- Officers' careers can be found in WO 76.
- Officers in the Navy can be found at ADM 196.

- Royal Navy Ratings for 1873 to 1924 can be found in ADM 188. The archives publish a guide 'Royal Naval Ratings guide 1853 to 1928' to help with the search.

Your ancestor may have been the widow of a Boer War Soldier. As we saw in the text many remarried soon after the death of their husband. You may find both the original name and their 'remarried name' in the National Archives, Transvaal Widows Fund if they made an application for help. PIN 96/23

Some of these regiments listed above have disappeared or amalgamated over time but today many regiments have their own museums and archives which you can visit. Many will undertake research on payment of a contribution as they operate as charities.

The Ogilby Trust is a charity which supports all the 136 regimental and corps museums of the British army in the UK. Its website gives a good general guide to looking for soldier ancestors. It does advise relatives to try and ascertain which regiment their ancestor served in. This could be possible through attestation papers or unit photos. Searching the Forces Records Website may help.

Army Museums Ogilby Trust,
58, The Close,
Salisbury, SP1 2EX
01722 3321888
diamot@armymuseums.org.uk

Many regiments kept their own journals which would include the period of Boer War. They may include names and stories of individual soldiers.

The Brigade of Guards keep their own records from the early nineteenth century to the present. Application to them must be by letter to:

Looking For Your Boer War Ancestor

Regimental HQ,
Grenadier/Coldstream/Scots/Irish Welsh Guards,
Wellington Barracks,
Birdcage Walk,
London, SW1E 6HQ

If your ancestor worked in the medical services, whether as a doctor or orderly, you need to approach the Army Medical Museum at Aldershot. Most of their records are after the First World war but it may be helpful for someone whose service overlapped that period. They can be contacted on 01252 868612. The archives@amsmuseum.co.uk forces website keep records on medical staff.

There are many museums and archives around the country including those under the umbrella of the Ogilby Trust who hold archives or have information on the war. One of the most helpful to me in my research was that of the Lancashire Fusiliers in Bury which provided the story and photo (front cover) of Private Kelly and access to the family stories of John Welsford and Henry Raven. So many of the Lancashire Fusiliers fought and died at the Battle of Spion Kop.

The Scots provided a large part of the British Army that fought in the Boer War. The Black Watch Regiment were major participants in the terrible Battle of Magersfontein in December 1899. Their museum is at:

Balhousie Castle,
Hay Street,
Perth, PH1 5HR
Tel: 01738 638152

Of the other major Scottish regiments there are:

The Highlanders Museum,
Fort George,
near Inverness
0131 310 8757 for research enquiries

The Gordon Highlanders,
St Lukes,
Viewfield
Aberdeen, AB15 7XH
01224 311200
research@gordonhighlanders.com

In Wales there are:

The Regimental Museum of the Royal Welsh in Brecon
01874 613310
info@royalwelsh.org.uk

Royal Welsh Fusiliers Museum
Caernarfon
LL55 2AY

The National Army Museum, Chelsea houses the Templar Research Centre which has the most comprehensive range of material on the Boer War. Currently it is closed for a major renovation but is due to reopen in 2016.

Devon Heritage at www.devonheritage.org is a very useful site for those with soldier ancestors in Devon. It lists memorials in the county to the Boer War and other conflicts. It has also traced brief biographies of some individual soldiers. The site owners are Muriel and Richard Brine and they can be contacted at editor@heritage.org.

Many local museums will have a display and some information on the Boer War.

Looking For Your Boer War Ancestor

The online Boer War Forum can answer questions on battles, individual soldiers. It has discussion forums which can be very informative.

There are many memorials to the war. Some are statues and some plaques in churches and schools. Names can be found through county or town records on the Roll of Honour website named above. Many cathedrals including Exeter, Truro, Hereford and Sherborne Abbey list soldiers from local regiments who died. The only completely comprehensive list is in a book by Sir James Gildea, now out of print, but published in 1912. A copy can be seen at SSAFA's Archives.

4, St Dunstans Hill,
London, EC3R Tel: 0207 403 8783
To make an appointment contact Juliette.c@ssafa.org.uk

The archives also contain lists of families which the organisation helped. They are anonymised but are quite specifically local may help you find a relative.

I had a great deal of help from the Archivist of Brighton Boys' Grammar School with stories of individual boys who fought. I suspect other grammar schools have such records so try approaching your ancestor's old school.

www.britishhomechildren.com is the website for the society helping people trace ancestors who were sent to Canada as home children. Many children were orphaned in this conflict and I found two groups sent to Canada in this way. It's possible that there were more. The migration did take place over a long period of time but the society estimates that some 10 per cent of Canada's population may be descended from these migrant children. Contact them at info@britishhomechildren.com

All of these sources should be of help to people who are aware of their connections to an ancestor who served in the war.

Given the number of men involved in this conflict it is quite likely that there are people who have connections they are not aware of. If you have gone into your family history and find that the 1901 census has a young married woman but no husband in the household it is quite likely that the husband is away fighting in South Africa. If he was subsequently killed or died in the war you may find that in the 1911 census the widow has remarried. I discovered my great uncle Robert Millburn, who was in the Coldstream Guards, in this way.

Finally some men who'd served in the military or were working in ancillary occupations such as telegraph operators decided to stay on after the war. There are some South African sites which may help you search for your ancestors. My Heritage www.heritage.com/archive-search Family Search.org gives access to many records

It is interesting that after the Boer War, Sir Alfred Milner, the Governor, and the Duke of Westminster proposed a scheme to resettle British soldiers on farms in an area which is now in the Free State. It was a large area from Thabu Nchu east of Bloemfontein to Wepener almost on the border with what is now the Kingdom of Lesotho. Any descendants may be traced through the above sites or through the Archives of the Free State in Bloemfontein.

ACKNOWLEDGEMENTS

I would like to thank the following people for sharing the stories of their relatives which have brought the history of the Boer War to life.

Roy Tucker: Albert Skedgell
Jenny Ridd: Fred Griffin
Dave Galley: Thomas Galley
Maureen Noonan: James Boseley, James Candy, Elizabeth Candy and the children of John Welsford and George Ravenhill
David Whitehead: Robert Slattery
Betty Booth who donated the diary of the Natal stretcher-bearer, Mr. Curnow
Carol Ruddock: Charles Henry Ruddock
Greville Wilson: Arthur Wilson's story
Dave Ecclestone, for providing the satirical footballing account by his grandfather, Reuben Evans
Mel Francis: W. H. Francis
Maureen Hunt for transcribing two poems by Thomas Bratt, the Portobello Poet
Mark Gillingham, archivist of Brighton Grammar school, for letters from Old Boys serving in the British Army
Dave Burn: Henry Arthur Burn
John Shalice: Henry Gardner
David Yabsley: Charles Dunn
Roger and Shirley Hannaford: Alfred Whitby
Sheilagh Stones: James Homeyard
Nigel Lutt provided the stories of Henry Goodwin and Henry

Cooper, residents in Cottage Homes
Graham Knight: Private Martin Nolan
Gordon Smith: Andrew Ernest Smith
Maurice Meardon: John Meardon
Malcolm Reynolds: Harry Churchill Beet
Louise Young: Samuel Young
Lynn Bagg: Trooper Burbridge
Elizabeth Rintoul: Donald Micklejohn
Brian Hall: Jesse Hall
Adrian Taylor: George Taylor
Norman Wilcock: William Wilcock
Barbara Vermeulen: William and Charles Gill
Malcolm Duncan: William Nielsen
Robert Messenger: Charles Henry Messenger
Doreen Cardew: Herbert John Browning
Nicola Wills: John Ball
Sheila Harding: Dr William Ashford
Phil Densham: William Coldridge
Robert Wall: Thomas Randell
Darren Hands : Frederick Hands

I would like to thank the following for their help with this book:

My husband Tony Marchese for all his support from proof-reading to accompanying me to South Africa for research purposes.
My sons Ricky and Daniel Marchese Robinson for their support and interest in this work.
Jenny Ridd for giving me the story of her great-uncle, Fred Griffin and becoming my friend with a major interest in history
Katie Mooney, Historian from Cape Town who linked me to their archives and photos.
Maureen Noonan from Accrington, Lancashire, amateur genealogist extraordinaire who helped unearth the stories of

Acknowledgements

several soldiers and families.

Simon Fowler for his information about charities at the time of the war.

Ian McGraw, historian from Dundee who has discussed ideas and made suggestions for the book.

Malcolm Duncan from Dundee who gave me the story of his grandfather and ongoing support and ideas.

Iain Flett and his team at Dundee City Archives who helpfully researched materials and always answered my questions.

Juliet Chapman, SSAFA Archives who donated research material.

Clare Gibson, The Army Children's Archives who contributed interesting pieces of history.

Raymond Heron, historian, Spion Kop Lodge, South who told us the story of Spion Kop within the context of South African history.

Jen Newby, previously at Pen and Sword, who inspired this project and gave me much ongoing support

Eloise Hansen, Pen and Sword who continued that support seamlessly.

NOTES

CHAPTER 1: A TALE OF TWO WARS
1. Mearns, Reverend Andrew. *The Bitter Cry of Outcast London*. (London Congregational Union, 1883).
2. Higgs, Michelle. *Tracing your Servant Ancestors*. (Pen & Sword, 2012), p.56.

CHAPTER 2: 'IT'LL ALL BE OVER BY CHRISTMAS'
1. From *Staines and Egham News*, October 1899. Display at Egham Museum.
2. Carver, Lord. *The National Army Museum Book of the Boer War*. (Sidgwick and Jackson, 1999), p.38.
3. Stewart Ross, *Dundee Courier and Argus* for soldiers' names from Battle of Magersfontein, reproduced 11 December 2014.
4. *Daily Telegraph* Shilling Fund: The National Archives (TNA) NSC 21/501.
5. Pakenham, Thomas. *The Boer War*. (Weidenfeld and Nicholson 1979), p.184.
6. *Daily Telegraph* Shilling Fund: TNA NSC 21/501.
7. Treves, Sir Frederick. *Diary of a Field Hospital*. (Cassel and Co, 1900), p.11.
8. Heward W.H. 'Siege of Ladysmith'. Sheffield Local Studies Centre 968:L SSTF.
9. Poem found in the papers of Lance Sergeant Staton, 'Diary of the Boer War 1899-1902': Rotherham Archives 578-K/2/7/7.

CHAPTER 3: THE CALL FOR VOLUNTEERS AND THE BESIEGED TOWNS
1. Recruitment of the Imperial Yeomanry, TNA WO 32/7866.
2. Alfred Lewis Collett, 'Battle of Spion Kop, 24 January 1900',

Boer War Diary.
3. From Winston Churchill's contemporary writing about the Battle of Spion Kop, reproduced in the *Mail Online*, 17 June 2010.
4. James Candy's letter from *Blackburn Weekly Standard and Express*, 24 February 1900.
5. Treves. *Diary of a Field Hospital*.
6. William Ward, Patient records London Hospital.
7. Murray, Captain Mary. *All the World*. (Salvation Army, 1901).
8. Letters of Thomas Stones, Preston Archives DDX2381.
9. F. Bennet letter to brother Charlie, Plymouth and West Devon Records Office 261/2
10. Mick Gallagher, Liverpool Archives 920 GAL.
11. Albert Theaker, Sheffield Archives LD 2411.

CHAPTER 4: THE WAR AT HOME
1. Courtesy Simon Fowler, 1999.
2. Paget, Julian. *No Problem too Difficult: A History of the Forces Help Society and Lord Roberts Workshops*. (SSAFA, 1979), p.2.
3. Hypatia Trust, History 51. Emily Hobhouse Workshop, Liskeard, 16 November 2013. Eleanor Tench and Jennifer Hobhouse Baulme.

CHAPTER 5: THE SICKNESS TOOK THEM
1. Denis Devine – Lancashire Fusiliers Annual Report.
2. Private Ince – from Lancashire Heritage site Past Forward from LT August 2003.
3. Private Shortland, Sheffield Local Studies 968.2 SSTF.
4. Private Charles Ireland from 'By Jingo' – Totnes Archives.
5. Diary of a Nurse working at Bloemfontein Hospital, National Army Museum. This was shown to me as a new acquisition by Dr A. Massie of the Museum.
6. West Wales Memorial Project – Steven John.

CHAPTER 6: AND THE BOYS WENT TOO
1. Liverpool League of Well Doers Collection. Liverpool Archives, M364 LWD 17/1.
2. Records of Boys from the Foundling Hospital A/FH/A/12/010/059-062 and Coram Foundation.
3. Carol Harris, Social History Editor at the Coram Foundation.

CHAPTER 7: THE BITTER END
1. Nasson, Bill, and Grundlingh, Albert. *The War at Home, Women and Families in the Anglo-Boer War.* (Tafelberg, 2013).
2. 'By Jingo', Totnes Archives.
3. Worth, Jennifer. *Shadows of the Workhouse.* (Orion Books and William Morris Publishers, USA, 2009), pp.253–4.
4. Hall, John. *That Bloody Woman: A Biography of Emily Hobhouse.* (Truran Books Ltd, 2008).

CHAPTER 8: 'A LAND FIT FOR HEROES'?
1. Dundee City Archives,
2. Wirksworth Commemorations from *High Peak News*, 18 October 1902.
3. Letters of Thomas Stones, Preston Archives DDX2381.
4. *Hansard* 1906.
5. Hackney Archives .
6. Jones, Edgar. *Historical Approaches to Post Combat Disorders.* (Institute of Psychiatry, Kings Centre for Military Health Research, London, SE5 9RJ).
7. Ibid.
8. War disability pensions, TNA PIN 15/3079.
9. Nigel Lutt, *The Wasp*, Journal of the Bedfordshire and Hertfordshire Regiment.
10. Letters of Thomas Stones, Preston Archives DDX2381.
11. Knight, Graham. *Fighting with the Royal Welsh Men of the Midlands in the Royal Welch Fusiliers 1900–1919.* (RWF Museum, Caernarfon).

12. Devon Heritage Centre, Records of Exminster Asylum.

CHAPTER 9: SUFFER LITTLE CHILDREN
1. Royal Victorian Asylum for Girls (Wikipedia).
2. Reference for Royal Victoria School in TNA PIN 96.
3. Edward VII contribution to reopened Transvaal Widows' and Orphans' Fund 21 July 1904 TNA PIN 96.
4. Criteria for widows receipt of payments TNA PIN 96/15, Appendix VI.
5. The British Home Children and Child Migrants to Canada is the present-day society that chronicles the lives of the migrants and descendants and campaigns on their behalf. The quote about their history and conditions comes from the British Home Children Advocacy and Research Association website Home Page.
6. Ravenhill, Louise. *Move Smart, Boy: A Novel about Home Children in Rural Prince Edward Island, 1911-13.* (Luika, 2002).
7. Lancashire Fusiliers Annual Report, 1900.

BIBLIOGRAPHY

Carver, Lord. *The National Army Museum Book of the Boer War.* (Sidgwick and Jackson, 1999).

Crowden, James. *From Ladysmith to Archangel, The Language of War Volume One: The Boer War 1899-1902.* (Flagon Press, 2013).

Hall, John. *That Bloody Woman: A Biography of Emily Hobhouse.* (Truran Books Ltd, 2008),

Mearns, Reverend Andrew. *The Bitter Cry of Outcast London.* (London Congregational Union, 1883).

Murray, Captain Mary. *All the World.* (Salvation Army, 1901).

Nasson, Bill. *The Boer War, the Struggle for South Africa.* (The History Press, 2011).

___, and Grundlingh, Albert. *The War at Home, Women and Families in the Anglo-Boer War.* (Tafelberg, 2013).

Paget, Julian. *No Problem too Difficult: A History of the Forces Help Society and Lord Roberts Workshops.* (SSAFA, 1979).

Pakenham, Thomas. *The Boer War.* (Weidenfeld and Nicholson, 1979).

Ravenhill, Louise. *Move Smart, Boy: A Novel about Home Children in Rural Prince Edward Island, 1911-13.* (Luika, 2002).

Treves, Sir Frederick. *Diary of a Field Hospital.* (Cassel and Co, 1900).

Worth, Jennifer. *Call the Midwife.* (Orion Books, 2009).

___. *Shadows of the Workhouse* (Orion Books, 2009).

INDEX

3rd Dragoon Guards, the 86–7
6th Dragoon Guards, the 86–7
6th Dragoons (Inniskillings), the 88
18th Hussars, the 32, 87, 143

Aberdeen Weekly Journal, the 66
Abbott, Mr and Mrs 128, 129
'Absent-Minded Beggar, The' 65, 66
Absent-Minded Beggar's Fund, the 61
Accrington 37
Admiralty, the 141
African population 108
agricultural depression 106
Akehurst, Hubert 97
Alexandra, Queen 104, 115
Alhambra Music Hall 65–6
Alleman Railway Siding 95
Apartheid Regime, the 99
armoured train 26
Ashanti Campaign, the 133
Ashford, Dr William 145
asylums
　Exminster 119
　The Royal Patriotic Asylum for Girls, 121
　Winson Green Lunatic Asylum 119

Attrill, Mrs 53
Australians 81

Baden-Powell, Robert 54, 55
Balfour, Prime Minister Arthur 108
Ball, John 145
Barnett, Louisa 24–5
Barnado's 116, 135, 136
Basutos 63
BBC, the 92
Bedfordshire Regiment, the 117
Beet, Harry Churchill 138
Belfast, South Africa 152
Belgian refugees 1
Belgium 151
Belmont 18, 152
Bennett, F. 50
bereaved families 107
bereaved mothers 30
Bermuda 99
Bethlehem 2, 96, 97, 140
Bideford 132, 134–5
Binyon, Lawrence 5
Birdsong 5
Birmingham 118
Birmingham Mail, the 125
Birmingham Post, the 58
Birmingham Town Hall 73
'Bittereinders', the 100

173

Blackburn 47
Blackburn Rovers 104
Black Watch, the 19, 152
'Black Week' 23, 56
Blanche, HMS 150
Bleach, Private Frank 79
Bloemfontein 2, 54, 56–7, 75, 77, 86, 113, 145
Bloomsbury Group, the 104
Boer commandos 91, 96
Boer families 91
Boer guerrillas 117
Boer rifles 40
Boer War, the 3, 5–6, 10–11, 86, 137, 140, 142–3, 147–9, 154
Booth, Charles 105
Bosanquet, Helen 69
Boseley, James 38, 114, 115
Bowcombe, Lizzie 80
Bowlby, Anthony 113
Boxing Day (1901) 140
Boys' Reformatory 116
Brandfort 95
Bratt, Thomas 56, 58
Breakfast Fund, the 109
Brighton Grammar School 19, 60, 74, 97
Bristol Mercury, the 67
British Empire, the 94
British Legion, the 129
British Home Children and Child Migration, Canada 126
Bromford Mills 125

Bronkhurst Spruit 74
Browning, Herbert John 144
Buchanan, Captain 15
Buller, General Sir Redvers 25, 40, 43, 50, 57, 118, 125, 150
Burbridge, Trooper 140
Burlington 153
Burn, Henry Arthur 63
Burnley 115
Bury 115
Bushwill, Francis 143

Call the Midwife 93
Camborne 142
Canada 153
Canadian Army 138
Canadian Embassy 136
Canadians 81
Candy, Elizabeth 123
Candy, James 42, 44
Canon Hill Park 2
Cape St.Vincent 60
Cape Town 53, 94
Carr, Police Constable 110
Carver, Lord 19
Castletown 141
Census of 1901 137
Census of 1911 136
Chamberlain, Joseph 73
Charity Organisation Society 69
Chelsea Hospital 114
'Chevril' 48
Ceylon 37, 99

Index

child care policies 136
Child Migration Schemes 126, 135
childrens' names 58
Chinese crisis 104
Chipping Norton 129
Christian, Prince 70, 71, 147
Christian, Princess 70
Christmas Day 96, 98
Churchill, Winston 7, 42, 76
City Imperial Volunteers, the 74
Cockerill, Major 77
Coldridge, William 150
Colenso 18, 24, 125, 148
Collet, Albert 41
Collet, Joseph 92, 154
concentration camps 7, 90, 96, 154
  for blacks 94
Coram, Thomas 85
Cornishman, The 142
cotton trade 105
  industrial slump 108
Coldstream Guards, the 3, 80, 103, 152
Commonwealth, the 99
Comrade Jim poem 111
Cooper, Henry 117
court martial 119
Courtney, Leonard, MP 72
Cranwells 116
Crimean veterans 130
Crimean War, the 68, 121

Cronshaw, Jimmy 104
Cuckfield 79
Curnow, Mr 25, 140, 148

Daily Graphic, the 109
Daily Mail, the 47, 69, 72
Daily News, the 68
Daily Telegraph Shilling Fund, the 21, 24, 69
Dardenelles, the 147, 151
Darwen 43, 123
Davison, John, MP 128
demobbed soldiers 108
Derbyshire Regiment, the 138, 144
Devon 21
Devonport 133, 146
Devonport Park 2
Devonshire Regiment, the 24, 38, 116
Distinguished Conduct Medal, the 150
Diamond Hill 152
disabled soldiers 107
disordered action of the heart (DAH) 113, 117
Divine, Denis 74, 113
Dore, Madame 67
Dorset Yeomanry, the 139–40
Doris, HMS 146
Douglas, Mr 128
Doyle, William 86
Drakensberg 28
Dublin Fusiliers, the 27

175

Duchy of Cornwall, the 145
Duke of Cambridge, the 68
Duke of York, the 125, 138
Duke of York's Military
  School, the 83
Duncan, William Neilson 143
Dundee 15, 20, 101, 143, 151
Dunn, Charles 80
Drummer Boy at Colesberg,
  the 84
Durban 43, 61, 101
Durham Light Infantry, the 87

East Kent Regiment, the 33,
  53, 86
Edward VII, King 142
  Coronation of 139
Elandslaagte 15, 102
Elands River 98, 140
enteric fever 30, 76, 79, 118,
Estcourt 42
eugenics 127
Evans, Ruben 51
Exeter 100, 108
Exeter Cathedral 143
Exeter Cathedral Memorial 22
Exeter Gazette, the 38

Farewell to Arms, A 5
Fellowes, Lieutenant Navarine
  76
Fielding, Trooper 45
First World War, the 4, 127,
  137, 141, 144, 146–7, 150, 152

Folland, Clara 133
Fort George 141
Foster, Captain 19
Forster's Education Act (1870)
  7, 65
Foundling Hospital, the 85
Francis, W. H. 53–4, 144
Frere 26
Fugler, Private 24

Gallagher, Mick 50
Galley, Thomas 35, 91
Gallipoli 5, 15
Gandhi, Mahatma 42
Gardner, Henry 76
Gell, Captain Pole 103
German East Africa 144
Gilchrist, Dr and Mrs 136
Gildea, Colonel Sir James 70
Gill, William and Charles 142
Godfrey, Sergeant T. 19
Goodwin, Henry 117
Gordon Highlanders, the 15
Gowongo Minstrels, 66
Gowrie, Private Thomas 19
Graspan, 18
Grey, Private 21
Griffin, Fred 21, 33, 35, 43,
  149
Griffiths, Trevor 92
Groenkop, Battle of *see*
  Tweefontein
Guardians, Poor Law 107
Guthrie, Dr 85

Index

Hackney 108,109
Hackney Board of Guardians 109
Haldane, Mr, Secretary of State for War 107
Hall, Jesse 141
Halwell 80
Hampshire Telegraph and Naval Chronicle, The 58
Hampstead Heath 110
Hands, Frederick, 150
Hardie, Kier 72, 108
Hardy, Thomas 32
Harrismith 140
Hatherleigh 138
Hay, Claude MP 107
Hayes, Sergeant 24
Hayes Wharf 140
Hazelbrae Memorial 136
Heward, W. H. 29, 33, 43, 48, 75
Highland Regiments 19
Hill, Octavia 69
Hobbs, Percy 34
Home Children 127, 128
Home for Catholic Friendless Youths, the 85
Homeyard, James 32, 110, 112
Hopton Hall 103
horses 151

Imperial Yeomanry, the 33, 34, 90, 96, 97, 98, 99, 138

Ince, Private, 75
India 118, 138
Industrial Schools 83
influenza 150
Inniskillings, the, *see* 6th Dragoons
Intombi 76
Ireland, Private Charles 77, 92
Irwin, Elsie, Red Cross nurse 145
Islandlwana 12
Isle of Wight 67

Jackson, D. I. 125
Jago, Bessie 116
Jameson, Leander 13
Jameson Raid, the 13, 68
Jardine, Robert 87
Johnstone, Morris 151
Jones, Professor 77
Joyce, Private 24
Jutland, Battle of 147, 151

Kaye, William 86
Keates, William 87
Kekewich, Colonel 22
Kelly, Patrick 45, 114
Kimberley 17, 18, 29, 37, 49, 148
King's College, London 78
Kingsbridge, 147
Kingsbury School 129
Kirkwood, Private 21
Kitchener, Lord 54, 90, 91

Kitchener's Fighting Scouts 143
Knowles, Captain Lees 130
Komatie Poort, 81
Kruger, Paul 12

labour colonies,109
labourers, 104
Labour Exchanges 109
Labour movement, the 108
Ladysmith 17, 29, 30, 38, 43, 48, 53, 66, 85, 144, 148, 150
Laing's Nek, 144
Lancashire, 103,105
Lancashire Fusiliers, the 41, 44, 74, 104,130
Lancashire Fusiliers' Compassionate Fund, the 132, 134
Lee, Jenny 94
Lewis, Charles 150
Lewisham Industrial School 84
Liberal Government, the 90
Light Infantry, 2nd Battalion The 86
Liskeard 72, 144
Littlejohn, Grace 133
Liverpool, 50, 66, 135
Liverpool Mercury, the 37, 67
Lloyd George, David M P 72, 73, 144
Local Government Board, the 109

locomotor ataxy 130
Logan, Charlotte 133
Lombards Kop 62
London 105
London, Jack 105
London Gazette, the 125
London Metropolitan Archives, the 1
London Morning Post, the 42
Long, Colonel 125
Lord Mayor of Birmingham, 128
Lord Mayor of London Fund, the 67, 68
Loyal North Lancashire Regiment, the 36
Lydenberg, 81, 150

Macclesfield Industrial School 85
Macmillan, Private J. 19
Mafeking 17, 54, 55, 57, 73
Magersfontein, 2, 101, 99, 118, 151
Maidstone 115
Majuba 12
Mann, Moses 24
Marlborough, HMS 147
McCrae, John 5
Meardon, John 138
Mearns, Andrew 8
Measles 91
Meiklejohn, Donald 141
Messenger, Charles Henry 144

Index

Methuen, Colonel 99
Middlesborough 67
Millburn, Robert 152
Milner, Governor James 36, 61, 142
Modder River 19, 49, 75, 95, 152
Molesworth, Miss Mary 134
Mooi River 43
Moore, Carrie 143
Morgan, Albert Peter 56
Mounsfield, Leslie 63
Mourant, R. W. 60, 64, 71
Murrask, Private 24
Murray, Captain Mary 46, 70, 77, 105

Naauyport 53
Natal Volunteer Ambulance Corps, the 25
National Army Museum, the 81, 95
National Unemployed Committee, the 108
National Women's Monument, Bloemfontein 154
'natives', Mafeking 55
Nechells, 124
Neill, W .M. 55, 56
Nelspruit 63
Nesbit, Enid 104
Netley 114
New Zealand 81

Newbridge, Ireland 84
Newcastle, South Africa 131
Nolan, Martin 117, 118, 119
Noonan, Maureen 128
North Devon Archives, the 135
North Staffordshire Regiment, the 86
North Wales 66
Northcote, Sam 36
Norvals' Point 54
Nottingham Castle 139
Nottinghamshire 153

Oliver Twist 125
Orange Free State, the 12, 89, 144
orphanages, 83, 135
Owen, Wilfred 5
Oxfordshire, 127

Paardeberg 117
Padstow 66
Paget, Julian 71
Parsons, Joe 80
Payne, Alfred 109
Pembroke 132
Pearsall, Ada and Luke 136
People of the Abyss, The 106
Pengelly, Corporal 24
Perth 101
Penzance 142
Piggots, Thomas 142
Phitis 115

Pietermaritzburg 46
Plaatje, Sol 54
policeman, military 119
Poor Law (1834) 9, 107, 121,
Poor Law Unions, London 109
Poor Relief 107
Plymouth 50, 146
Port Elizabeth 144
Portuguese East Africa 145
Post-Traumatic Stress 112
Powis, Robert 88
Preston, 131
Pretoria 38, 54, 74, 81, 89, 94, 154
Priestley, J. B. 106
Prince Edward Island 128
Prince of Wales, the 70
Printy, Edward 16
Pro-Boers, the 72 ,73, 154
Prothero, Captain 18
Punjab, the 138

Quebec 135
Queen's Pipe, the 139
Queen's Royal Rifles, the 141, 142
Queen's Shilling 83
Quiller-Couch, A. T. 73

'Ragged One Hundred', the 49, 148
Randell, Thomas 150
Raven, Catherine 131
Raven, Henry 44, 131

Raven, Emily 131
Ravenhill, George 25, 125, 138
Ravenhill, George jnr 128, 29
Ravenhill, Lilly 128, 129
Ravenhill, Louise 128
Ravenhill, Raymond 128, 129
Red Cross Society, the 68
Redruth 142
Reeves, Alice 147
refugee camps 90
Reid, Dr Geoffrey 97
Riefontein, Battle of 16
Roberts, Freddie 25, 125
Roberts, Lord 25, 81, 90, 125
Robinson, Alice 152
Robinson, Ellen 72
Rondebosch 113
Roodeport 143
Rooival 139
Rorkes Drift 12
Rosenannon Methodist Church 145
Rowntree, Seebohm 105
Royal Army Medical Corps (RAMC), the 19, 78, 113
Royal Artillery Cottages 116
Royal College of Surgeons, the 145
Royal Engineers, the 143
Royal Field Artillery, the 86
Royal Fusiliers, the 144
Royal Hibernian Military School, the 39
Royal Naval Hospital, the 147

Index

Royal Navy, the 17, 38
Royal Patriotic Fund, the 68, 70
Ruddock, Charles Henry 49, 148
Rustenberg, 96

Salvation Army, the 108, 126
Sanaas Post 75
Sandringham Estate 115
'Savage South Africa' exhibition 61
Seager, Noel 19, 79
Second World War, the 142
Semley, Dorset 139
Schmidt, Ernest 137
'Scorched Earth' Policy 2, 90, 91
Scott, Captain 22
Scottish Horse Regiment, the 141
Scots Greys, the 49, 149
Scullion, Thomas 19
Sheffield 62
Sherborne Abbey 82
Shortland, Private J. E. 62, 76
servants, 104
shrapnel 27
Shropshire Light Infantry, the 87
Simonstown 17
sjambok 64
Skedgell, Albert 17, 146
Slattery, Robert 36, 55

Smart, Henry 86
Smit, Chris 13
Smith, Andrew Ernest 137
Smith, Harry 102
Smith, Private J. 19
Snow Hill Station 118
Social Democratic Federation 108
Soldiers' Effects Fund, the 132
'Soldiers of the Queen' 67, 101
SSAFA 66, 68, 70
Somerset 142–3
South African Rifles, the 144
South Lancashire Regiment, the 42
Southampton 115
Southgate, Walter 108, 109
soup kitchens
   Lancashire 108
   Mafeking 55
Soft Nose 79
Sparkes, George 87
Spearman's Farm 44
Spion Kop, Battle of 2, 39, 44, 46, 47, 48, 76, 93, 104, 115, 117, 118, 123, 130, 131, 141, 148
Springfontein 78, 96
Staffordshire 103
Staffordshire Militia, the 56
Staffordshire Regiment, the 49
Staines and Egham News, the 16

Standerton Stationary
    Hospital 81
Stanley, Lieutenant Colonel
    128
Staton, Lance Sergeant W. 30
Stead, W.T. 72
Steyn, President 51, 154
Stones, Thomas 47, 94, 104,
    117
Stop and Rest Inn, the 48
Stormberg Junction 18
Stroud 137
suicide 111–13
Sussex Daily News, the 97
Sussex Regiment, the 79

Talana Hill 15
Tatham, Edward 87
Tavistock 24
Taylor, George 141
Tenerife 61
Territorial Army, the 145
Thabu Nchu 151
Theaker, Albert 60
Thomas, Edward 5
Thomas, Dr G. Danford 110
Thorneycroft, Lieutenant
    Colonel 40
Tierney, Private 77
Tilson, Phillip 87
Toronto, distribution centre
    136
Tom's Tenement 145
Topsham 145

Totnes 103
Totnes Times, the 38
Trades Council, the 108, 109
Trafalgar Square 108
Transvaal 89, 144
Transvaal Widows' Fund, the
    106, 122, 124, 132, 134
Treves, Sir Frederick 28, 44,
    114
Tugela Heights 144
Tugela River 28
Truth 67, 69
Tweebosch, Battle of 99
Tweefontein, Battle of 2, 96,
    97, 98, 140

Uitlanders, the 13
Ulundi 12
unemployment 108
Unemployment Benefit 109
Upstairs, Downstairs 9

Venterspruit 39, 48, 133
Vereeniging, Treaty of 99
Victoria, Queen 6, 13, 28
Victoria Square, Birmingham
    129
Vigers, Ernest Samuel 81
Vlakfontein 96
Voluntary Aid Detachment
    (VAD) hospital 146
Vryburg 22
Wagon Hill, 38, 39, 48, 115,
    116

Index

Wakkerstroom 138
War Office, the 107
Ward, Sir Robert 110
Ward, William 46
Warren, General 44, 118
Watling, 66
Watney, Lieutenant Jack 97
Webber, Charles 116
Webber, Private 73
Welsford, Ada 133, 134, 135
Welsford, Annie 132, 134, 137
Welsford, Clara 134
Welsford, John 39, 132
Welsford, William 133, 134, 135
Welsh Hospital 78, 96
Welsh Regiment, the 63, 86
West India Regiment, the 77
Westminster Abbey 129
Wet, Christian de 97
Whitby, Alfred 14
Whitechapel 106
White, General 29

Wignell, Samuel 86
Wilcock, William 142
Willenhall 50
Wilson, Arthur 49, 79, 83
Witton Cemetery 120, 128
Witwatersrand 13
Woolford, Hilda 150
Worcestershire Regiment, the 63
Workhouses 106, 107, 125, 126, 130, 135
Wrexham 118
Wriksworth 103
Wyke Regis 14

Yeatman, Charles 87
York 105,
York Minster, 72
Young, Samuel 139
Yserspruit 99

Zulus, the 11, 12